WHEN I WAS A PIE

AND OTHER SLICES OF FAMILY LIFE

M. L. FARB

CONTENTS

BAKING A LIFE PIE

For my parents,
who taught me through word and example
to follow Christ.

PREFACE

Most stories end with *Happily Ever After*. This one starts with it.

These are slices of life in the form of short stories, musings, comics, and poetry—showing bright moments, soul pondering, frustrations and side-aching laughter.

It is life, lived in the moment and observed.

Welcome to the eclectic joy we call our family.

～

Maria: The omniscient note-taker. Not really omniscient. If this was one of my novels—maybe. But in real life, even hindsight is less than 20/20. Definitely a note-taker. This book comes from millions of words hen-scratched on paper then typed into more readable journals.

Jesse: My best friend and collaborator in all things awesome and crazy. My balance.

Cherry: Artist extraordinaire and illustrator of this book.

Pecan: Our source of quotes, laughter, and unique points of view.

Apple: Everyone's, *everyone's*, best friend.

Lime: Lover of bugs and nature. Don't let him hand you a spider—he will, and it will be alive.

Huckleberry: Must have angels protecting him, because he's survived so many curiosity-induced injuries.

Strawberry: Sweet and determined. Her daddy's miniature.

. . .

* Names have been changed to pie flavors for your protection. If you knew them, you'd have to become family.

Our family, plus a few imaginary friends

~

This book is divided into "pies," each consisting of multiple years, with the following types of chapters:

- *Slices*: snapshots of life.
- *Baker's Tips*: lessons we've learned over the years in marriage and parenting. These are ones that work for us and hopefully will give you ideas of how to come up with your own life tips tailored to your specific circumstances.
- *Into the Oven*: the difficult experiences that have changed us, just as a pie changes in the oven's heat.

The last portion of the book, "Baking a Life Pie," is full of "ingredients:" daily and weekly actions that bring structure and joy to our life. Some of them are essential ingredients and some are fun bonus flavors.

Note: I belong to The Church of Jesus Christ of Latter-day Saints. My life experiences and thoughts are seen through that lens. However, any errors in this book are my own.

~

Story Pebbles

I collect stories the way a little boy collects pebbles,
picking them up along the gravel path of daily life:
the 'nothing events' that happen and get forgotten.

Toe-stubbing stories that I could kick away.
Phrases sparkling in the middle of mundane words.
"I'm covering his ears and I can still hear him."

I stuff them into the back pockets of my mind,
scatter them
on edges of envelopes
between phone numbers and to-dos;
filling notebook after notebook with hurried hen-scratch.
"The eyes in the back of my head can't see."

They tumble through my thoughts
joyful scattering unorganized,
rich soil for conversation and learning.
"I cut a crawl hole in the door."

I collect stories like pebbles.
My everyday nothings that are everything to me.

BEFORE PIE THERE WAS JAM

Summer of the New Roof

It was the summer after my older brother and I returned from Russia and before my younger brother headed to Italy. It was the summer before I got married, though I'd not yet had my first kiss. It was the last summer we'd all be home together.

I'm bookended by my brothers. I couldn't remember life without them. We'd grown through the years, building forts, climbing trees, canning applesauce, studying calculus, staying up to the yawning hours of the morning discussing books and ideas. We were the three amigos. Best friends. Confidants.

That summer I gained a new best friend. One who replaced my brothers as being my closest confidant. The three amigos became the four musketeers for that brief summer.

It was a summer of ends and beginnings. Dad decided it was a good summer to replace our roof.

—

As he had when digging out a fruit room, laying sod, or removing a dead tree, Dad organized our family into a learn-on-the-job workforce. Dad, my brothers—Bob and David—and I were to be the main muscle, though Mom and my little sisters joined in too.

The roof had been re-shingled on top of old shingles about five times. It was a beautiful old 4000-square-foot mansion of a house with three levels, and enough rooms for each of us five kids to have our own room if we wanted, though we often roomed together so we could host exchange students and foster kids. We also had a piano room, for teaching piano lessons, and a library. The roof was vast. The shingles layered densely.

Dad started by installing eye-bolts every ten or so feet along the ridgeline of the roof. We had a crash course in safety harnesses, ropes, and knots. Then we ascended to the roof, harnessed up, and started peeling layer upon layer of shingles with flat-nosed shovels and then tossing them off the edge of the roof to a waiting dumpster. We sometimes missed the dumpster. Our rosemary bush survived being crushed flat under shingles for several days.

I'd gone rappelling once, about ten years before. I liked climbing when I had three points of contact, meaning hands and feet. But with the harness, my three points became feet and harness. That first day on the roof I kept my focus on my feet staying firmly on the roof and hesitantly shoveled at the shingles. After an exhausting hour, I listened to Dad's urging, "Trust the harness, it will hold you." By day two I was standing at the edge of the roof, leaning with my full weight on the harness, flinging shingles into the dumpster. The ropes held.

Tearing off shingles was filthy work. We looked like chimney-sweeps: black hands, black faces. Or maybe coal miners with our harnesses and ropes, but instead of descending into the bowels of the earth, we ascended to the rooftop. My brothers were much stronger than I was, but I could work as long as they could—or so I claimed. I was exhausted at the end of each day. We traded our late-night sibling conversations for daytime banter over the scrape of shovels on shingles. It took us four days to get down to the plywood base, and then we had to take off most of the plywood because it had rotted.

My friend's older brother, Jesse, joined us. I hadn't seen him in two years. He was tall and lean with dark, wavy hair and a quick smile. Though he was twenty-one, most people thought he was sixteen because of his ageless, part-Japanese features. But then, many people thought I was fourteen, though I'd recently turned twenty. I was short compared to my siblings, flat chested, and still struggled with acne.

We were friends. We'd gone sledding and played mud football with our families. We competed against each other in stick pulls and leg wrestling. He was a fun part of the group. Like my brothers. Then he'd left for Germany and I'd headed to college and Russia. We'd kept in contact through letters. Two years was a long time, and I wasn't sure if I wanted to just be friends or hope for something more. It didn't help that every time he looked at me, he grinned and my face grew warm.

I turned my attention to the work. One of our first days working together, Jesse, Bob, and I pried away wooden siding so we could tuck tar paper under it. Jesse and I stood on two ladders with pry bars while Bob worked tucking in the tar paper from the roof. It was going well until my pry bar slipped and I split my lip. Jesse dropped his pry bar to the grass and offered me a hand down from the ladder.

"I'm fine," I insisted as I held my dirty sleeve to my bleeding mouth.

He dabbed my lip with a damp cloth. "You certainly are."

That broke the ice, though thankfully not a tooth. In the following weeks we chatted as we worked side by side. I told him about my marathon study of Greek warfare, desert landforms, and medieval Italian politics. These were for a novel I hoped to write. He asked questions and brainstormed story ideas. Characters took life between cutting plywood. He shared tales from his church mission, outlined video-game stories, and told jokes. Lots of jokes; mostly geeky, some groaners, and all fun.

My brothers joined in the joking, and our laughter grew as loud as the hammering. Then the four of us shifted gears to philosophy and talked about what we would perceive if the world were two-dimensional or four-dimensional.

Jesse fit into our eclectic conversations—delighting me with his insights. He and Bob took time to think before speaking, while David and I would rattle off words faster than a machine-gun.

Rain clouds gathered, and half our roof was open rafters. We worked through the night and until the next morning. By then we'd covered all the plywood with tar paper, then stapled blue tarps and white plastic over the other half of the roof. It looked like modern art—half tent, half house. But it was watertight and kept out the rain.

When the rain finally cleared, we finished covering the rafters with plywood and started shingling. Jesse had gotten another summer job that made it harder for him to come help. I missed him. My mornings and evenings whispered with fervent prayers, seeking guidance in what to do. I wanted to go to a university in a different state, but Jesse was staying in Oregon to attend school. Should I go, or should I stay?

God answered with peace. My father's words echoed in my mind, "Trust the harness. It will hold you." I leaned into the unknown future and signed up for classes at the local college. *Trust God. He will hold you.*

∿

Conversations with God

"Dear Heavenly Father, I like Jesse. He's sweet; he's a gentleman. But this is all so new. I've never felt this way about someone before. Please help me know what to do."

A gentle feeling of comfort rested over me, along with the thought, *move forward, ask questions, observe, get to know him.*

∿

Jesse took me to the movie *Lilo and Stitch*. Afterwards he mimicked Stitch perfectly: "I'm cute and fluffy." He's certainly cute. I laughed as I snuggled next to him.

"Dear Father, I really like him. How do I judge what kind of man he is?"

The next day as I listened to a church worldwide broadcast, one speaker talked about the qualities of a husband and another about righteous women. I took notes, decided what was important to me, and compared them to Jesse and me. God gave me tools to answer my own questions.

∿

Jesse and I ate lunch on a bench between classes. He took my hand. "What do you want to do with your life?" My mind stuttered. I had so many dreams and goals. He listened intently as I told of my desires for learning, creating, and family. Then he told me his own dreams, including ones he hoped I'd be part of.

"Father in Heaven, I've been observing Jesse and asking questions. He is honorable, has high standards and worthy pursuits. He's funny, sweet, and smart. He's a good son and brother in his family. He treats everyone with courtesy. He is, in so many ways, someone I can see spending the rest of my life with. And tonight he told me he loves me. He's wonderful and I love him. Why am I frightened?"

A phrase from the hymn "Lead, Kindly Light" whispered through my head. *"I do not ask to see the distant scene, one step enough for me."*

≈

"Oh wow! Heavenly Father, he asked me to marry him! I said yes! I love him! But I'm terrified. This isn't just for a day, or a year, or even a lifetime. I'm promising to stand beside him through the eternities. If Thou art pleased with this decision, please help me know."

Peace calmed my clenching stomach. The peace of God's "Yes."

≈

First Kiss

Sometimes the world turns upside down
and joy pours out like confetti,
leaving me tumbling through space,
dancing in the freefall.

≈

Father's Blessing

My father's hands lie warm on my head,
his voice soft and full of emotion.
I'm his first child to get engaged,
his oldest daughter.

The counsel flows:

Communicate.
Plan together.
Pray together.
Write down answers to your prayers.
Follow the promptings of the Holy Spirit.
Be not swayed by others.

He gave us tools to
weather intense storms.
Storms we little understood we'd face.

~

Marriage Advice

I received many pieces of advice as I prepared for marriage, some sweet, some funny, and some profound. But perhaps the most impactful emotionally was a piece that showed me another side of the man I was marrying.

A well-meaning acquaintance pulled me aside. "You really should wear makeup more often, or someday he may leave you."

Tears pricked in my eyes as I bit back a retort. *Do you think he only loves me because of my face? He's not shallow!*

As soon as I could escape, I found Jesse and asked him, "Do you think I should wear makeup more often?"

He gave me a quizzical look, mouth slightly open and eyebrows raised. "No. I'd rather kiss your skin than kiss paint. Why?"

I let go of a held breath. Her words had no basis. His words grounded me with reassurance.

He's proved true to his statement over the years. He's seen me at my visually worst with sleep deprivation and baby spit-up, and held me in a romantic embrace. He's seen me at my most elegant, and on those days our best kisses happened after I'd washed the paint off.

~

Temple Covenants

> Kneeling across from each other,
> in God's holy house.
> Hands clasped,
> making promises
> to each other,
> to God.

> Promises for today, tomorrow, and forever.

~

We are JaM

He is Jesse. I am Maria. Together we are JaM—two distinctly flavored friends who fell in love and merged our lives to become us. I'm still me. He's still he. Together we enhance each other's strengths and balance our weaknesses, making a zesty sweet match.

THE COLLEGE PIE

SLICE 1: GEEKING OUR FIRST YEAR

Home

One-bedroom apartment,
in a town two states away from family,
hunting for three pieces of furniture—
bed, table, desk. We can do without the rest.

No car.
One bike,
two sets of feet,
and campus only a block away.

Three job interviews.
Two stacks of college textbooks.
One quilt hung on the cinder block wall.
A blank journal to fill.

Two friends learning to be married.
Becoming one.

~

First Quarrel

It all started because we didn't know.
I didn't know what bugged him.
He didn't know what was important to me.

We both were tired,
stressed with school,
and so we quarreled.

A burst of words.
A storm of silence.
An hour of coldness.

Then we talked and listened,
and learned from each other:
what was important,
what drove us up the wall.

And made peace.
Until the next time.

"They made peace... But that did not prevent such quarrels from happening again, and exceedingly often too, on the most unexpected and trivial grounds. These quarrels frequently arose from the fact that they did not yet know what was of importance to each other...It was only in the third month of their married life...that their life began to go more smoothly."
    —*Leo Tolstoy*[1]

The truth of the honeymoon period. A joyful, awkward, beautiful time of learning who our other half is. And in doing so we became more clearly our unique selves as well as a united couple.

~

Acts of Love

A kiss, a hug, and "I love you" starts and ends each day and appears in the many moments in between.

Yes, we're newlyweds. Utterly, sappily, and unashamedly in love. We've worked to get here and we'll keep working to stay here.

Prayers said together, Scriptures studied side by side, long conversations, quiet times of just being, helping each other with homework—even if I don't understand engineering and music history is not his interest.

Patience. His patience with my desire to solve problems immediately. My patience when he's so focused that I feel invisible. Our patience with each other's different upbringings and expectations. Chagrin followed by shared laughter.

A geeky joke to savor over a dinner of rice, green beans, and canned salmon. Playing footsie under the table. Snuggles while watching Kim Possible or reading Lloyd Alexander. Asking about each other's day and really listening. My blush when he reminds me, as he has every day since before we got engaged, "You're so cute."

Daily acts of love.

~

Apartment Seasons

September

Sparrows nest in our
cinder block walls.
A cubby made larger by
birdsong only inches away.

November

Fourteen-inch icicles, growing longer. The heater clunks and roars its way through the day. At night we turn it off so we can sleep in silence, buried under blankets and homemade night caps pulled low around our ears. Soon it will be too cold for turning it off, and we'll learn to sleep through the noise. For now, we live like "The Night Before Christmas".

February

More snow this winter than most locals can remember. It is lovely to see the variations as snow drifts, spins, or gently floats down. The temperature isn't too cold, either—lows in the positive single numbers and highs in the 20s. It does make for slippery roads. I've seen or heard too many cars skid.

June

Logan's linden trees.
Honey-scented bane—asthma.
Windows shut so we can breathe.

≈

Study Buddies

The Maze

Jesse and I sit side by side on the carpeted floor studying a simple maze on graph paper. His computer programming homework is to create a program that can navigate any maze. We are brainstorming away from the computer.

He explains, "We need a recursive function to search for a path from a starting position and find the end or exhaust all possibilities. We also need to—"

"Um, what is a recursive function?"

"A function that calls itself so it can repeat as many times as needed."

"Oh, a loop." Bits and pieces from a high-school programming class come back to me. We talk through possibilities, using the graph paper to visualize what the program would do with a specific set of instructions.

We groan as we find places in the maze where our recursive function won't work and must figure out how to modify it. Finally our pencil makes it to the end of the paper maze following only the set looping instructions. I leave to work on my own homework as he sits down at the computer to write in a foreign language of FIND-PATH(startx, starty).

Developing Character

I lean forward, staring at the computer screen, resting my chin on my thumb and forefinger. The rough edges of a story dangle in between written words and imagined worlds. A character is giving me trouble.

Gentle arms wrap around my shoulders, pulling me back to earth. Jesse kisses my cheek. "Where's Halavant now?"

I lean into him, breathing in his scent. "Nowhere good."

He sets a chair next to mine. "Let's see if we can get him out of there." Jesse enters my novel's world, and together we fight the bandits of character inconsistencies and plot holes.

~

The Knight and the Squire

Sixteen credits of engineering.
Working to support our family.

Homework stretches into the night.
Months into the semester,
an endless month remaining.

Exhaustion evolves into strep throat,
a crushing blow to my knight.
He shoulders his classes
and trudges through each day.

I want to fight his battles for him,
but only he can attend his classes and take his tests.

So I act as squire:
help him prepare,
study beside him,
read his textbooks out loud when
exhaustion makes his eyes droop.

Knight and Squire,
side by side,
face the dragon semester.

And with God's help,
we not only survive,
but learn skills to
fight our next battles.

～

Cemetery Seasons

We lived a block away from campus. Our path to classes took us through the cemetery. It became my place of pondering and peace.

Cemetery in the Winter

I pull on a sweater,
button my wool coat,
and tuck the gray scarf
over my mouth and nose.

It's not quite as cold as in Russia,
but close enough.
Five-foot-long icicles hang from the eaves.

The trudge from our one-bedroom apartment to campus
is shorter through the cemetery.
A packed path cuts sharply between headstones.

Bare-branched trees bend under snow.
Pine green peeks from white blankets.
Beside my path, snow piles higher than my knees.

Here and there, smaller paths split off,
not to campus, but to grave markers.
Some are narrow but well packed;
others are just deep footprints.

Remembered love,
strong enough to break a path through cold.

I place my hand on my abdomen.
I'm not far enough along to feel a flutter.
A beginning, surrounded by many ends.

But are they ends?

Stone after grave marker after memorial proclaim otherwise:

Families are Forever

Cemetery in the Summer

A deep drone rumbles
across solid stones.
A kilted bagpiper walks the paths,
making evening glow with piped notes.
Tribute to the dead,
and call for the living to
remember.

Cemetery in the Autumn

Hand in hand,
my husband and I walk the cemetery.
I'm hugely pregnant.
A breeze cools us from our 90°F apartment.

Tombstone inscription:
With the help of the Lord,
We will always land on our feet.

Truth in stone,
though we stumble to live it.

〜

Geeking our first anniversary

A year of marriage,
a baby on the way,
wages saved
for the coming school year

How to celebrate?

A picnic at Willow Park—
a walk through the free zoo.
Marvel at the baby wallaby
and awkward adolescent swans.

Should we splurge at Magical Moon Toys?
Get a marble maze construction set?

It costs less than eating out
and will provide years of fun
for a growing family.

Already hours of fun.

We fill our table with
experiments on
gravity and relationships.

BAKER'S TIP: LESSONS LEARNED IN A
YEAR OF MARRIAGE

Be patient: with myself, with my husband, with us together.

Communicate: Jesse coined the phrase "geeking out together". It is when we talk about anything and everything—serious to silly. One of our favorite pastimes.

Pray together and pray for each other. Read Scriptures together. These are the best-spent minutes in a day.

God answers prayers in unexpected but wonderful ways.

Make decisions as a couple, after we've both studied it out and talked together. We don't have to agree about everything (because we don't), but we work it out together.

. . .

Big plans change. It's OK.

Fun doesn't require money. Housing and food do. Education is expensive. Be creative in the first, frugal in the second, and study hard in the third.

Marriage and education take daily effort. The rewards for both are more than worth it.

SLICE 2: CHERRY BLOSSOM

Creating while Creating

Two weeks after I started my most intensive semester of college, I found out we were expecting, something we'd been hoping for for months. Eight months later, I graduated with my bachelor's degree in Music and English Composition.

And then I graduated into motherhood.

The last of my formal education was filled with creating: composing and arranging music, writing a short memoir of a grandmother, drafting a novel, exploring poetry, plus all the readings, research papers, and tests that go with thirty labor-intensive credits. I loved learning and creating, and I was certain I'd never be so busy again in my life.

Little did I know that motherhood would take my creating, improvising, learning, and enduring to a whole new level. And a whole new joy.

~

Prenatal Perceptions

I'm a couple months pregnant with our first child and my husband writes his sister. "Can you believe that before the year ends, you will be an aunt? I suppose you would like to pose a similar question to me. All I can say is YES, YES, YES!!! I am very, wonderfully, absolutely excited! I love this whole eternal family thing; it is the most rewarding thing I have ever done. I'd scorn to change my place with kings; I couldn't ask for more."

—

Five months pregnant and I'm starting to show. We don't have a car, so he goes shopping with me and helps carry the groceries home on the bus. He listens as I chatter about my poetry class and the headaches of music composition.

∼

Pause

Sawtooth mountains,
home of cousin-forged memories,
trailless hikes to the top of Abe's Chair,
swims in glacier-melt lakes,
and wolf-sung campfires.

I'm eight months pregnant and
I want to capture years of moments.

Instead of the traditional hikes
and climbing the telephone pole,
I take long walks with my husband.
We see a golden eagle, owl, elk, and cranes.

Grandpa and Grandma tell stories,
times of before and lessons for ahead.
Experience from parents of eleven
to soon-to-be mom and dad.

We play dominoes, spoons, and Egyptian Ratskew.
Hands sometimes survive.
My sister and I compete across the air hockey table.
Two pucks ricochet, matching our wild laughter.

Jesse sits atop the swingset,
filling the air with plaintive tones
of his ocarina.

Time pauses, holding me,
before life pushes me forward
into motherhood.

∾

Baby Shower Advice

Many of my aunts, girl cousins, and friends gather to shower me with gifts and advice before I become a mother. Some are grandmothers, and some have yet to become mothers. My own mother lives twelve hours' drive away—too far to come for the party—but she will be here for my baby's birth.

- Be generous with praise and slow with criticism.
- Talk to your child about everything; as you cook, clean, or anything else.
- Never get angry with a child for acting his/her age.
- Ear mufflers might be nice for the noise.
- Let your children know that you love your spouse. Allow them to see you hug and hear your heartfelt praise. Give them confidence in your fidelity and strength in a family unit.
- It's okay if you get frustrated; every new mom does! Don't be afraid to ask for help. Remember both you and the baby are learning and adjusting to life.
- Cleaning the house while the kids are still growing... is like

shoveling the snow while it is still snowing! (It's important...
but challenging!)

- It is OK to cry with your baby.
- Always take the opportunity to bear your testimony to your children.
- Don't make your baby eat anything you wouldn't eat. It's cruel.
- Make sure you have a new diaper and wet wipes at hand *before* you take off the old one.
- Read to your children early. Read to them your favorites. Take them on your lap and tell stories of family and history, and about themselves.
- It's okay to be wrong. Being able to apologize to your children teaches them how to be humble, too.

And the two that made me laugh the most:

- Get a dog leash—actually I think they make kiddie ones now. We used one on my brother. It was useful. — *from a cousin*
- Don't put your baby on a leash. —*from another cousin*

~

Realization

My aunt said having a baby is the one time that realization is greater than the expectation. This is true.

~

Harvest Ball

New parents with six-week-old baby in tow,
we trudge through snow to the harvest ball.

Exhaustion from baby-nursing nights
and intense school days
melts under music.

We jive and spin to the
rich brass call of "Sing, Sing, Sing".

I float in his arms as we
trace the steps of Strauss' "Vienna Waltz".

We laugh our way through fast songs.
He has natural rhythm and style.
I follow in stumbling imitation.
"Walk like an Egyptian" and "Cotton Eye Joe"

I lay my head on his shoulder
to the gentle swaying of "Lady in Red".

Our baby watches from her car seat,
then begs to join.
We dance, her nestled between us,
until she falls asleep.

A limbo line starts.
I try my luck and startle to find that
pregnancy limbered my joints.
I skim under the stick at waist height.
He cheers me on.

We return to our dancing.
Two become one in music and movement.

Hours later we return home,
the dance making our steps light over snow
and our hearts ready for the coming struggles.

~

Generational Bonds

Cherry's Namesake

We name our firstborn after Jesse's grandmother. She has almond eyes like her namesake, though hers are blue while her great-grandma's are deep brown. We want our daughter to know of the courage and resilience of the woman who survived WWII, the atomic bomb, several cancers, living in a foreign country, raising five children, and through it all being a beacon of humor and joy.

Four Generations of Oldest Daughters

I stand holding my new baby next to my mom and her mom. We four are each the oldest daughters in our families. My grandma is a physicist, my mom a library scientist, I'm a writer. We each are wives, mothers, older sisters, curious learners, hard workers, and most importantly—followers of Christ. What will my daughter become?

~

Father's Love Song

Stanza One
1 a.m.
She's wide awake.
Daddy dances with her
to the silent music
of fatherhood.

Stanza Two
She splashes in three inches
of warm river water.
Daddy makes her a sand castle,
grinning as her splashes

run off his face.

Stanza Three
She rests in her car seat.
He crouches next to her and
whistles an ocarina's
gentle melody.

∾

Milestones and Moments

Doctors ask about milestones:
rolling, crawling, walking,
is the child on schedule?

Mothers see moments:
milky smiles, trilling cry,
giggles in her sleep.
Soft hand grasping my finger.
Bright eyes watching
a world brand new to her.

∾

First Birthday

Game One
"Open the presents."
She rubs her hands over the sparkly wrapping.
"Like this." Daddy guides her to pull apart the paper.
She grows distressed. It's ruining the pretty box.
Only when toy dishes appear does she calm.

Game Two

"Blow out the candle."
She squints her eyes and studies the flame.
"Like this." I blow on her cheek.
She turns and blows at me.

Game Three
What is this?
She stares at the piece of cake,
then picks off a crumb and another.
After five minutes of dainty eating,
she smashes the cake with her spoon.

~

Picky Eater?

Course I
Cherry refuses pasta and oatmeal.
She spits out meat and milk.
She tolerates a bite of green beans.
She's tiny with a fiery will.

Daddy eats rice with a seaweed paste.
She begs a taste.
Her eyes widen as her mouth closes around the
rice- and nori-laden chopsticks.
More, please!

Course II
Sourdough and rye,
sweet and sour meatballs.
She's not picky,
she's bored with bland.
She wants flavor!

~

The Siren

She runs happily screaming.
Our crystal vase hums in response.
Future opera singer?
If my ears can survive till then.

~

The meaning of "Dada"

She's eighteen months.
She draws, she pretends,
she puts together puzzles,
but she doesn't talk.

Then one night,
she points to Daddy and says, "Dada."
We cheer and clap.
She points to me and says, "Dada."
We laugh and repeat "Mama"
until she says it too, pointing to Daddy.

We point to each of us, "Dada," and "Mama."
Her eyebrows scrunch, as if to say,
"Why can't there be one word for the both of you?"

~

Attention

I sit at the computer, writing.
My toddler takes one of my hands

and kisses my palm.
She has my immediate attention—
melted heart and all.

~

Art from Words

A month shy of two years, Cherry gets through life with a few select words. To expand her vocabulary, I sit with a pencil and paper. "Cherry, tell me what to draw."

She grasps my pencil in perfect grip, the grip she'd developed before she could walk, and draws a circle with two little circles in it. "Eyes," she says, then adds two pointed triangles at the top of the large circle. "Kitty!"

A picture worth a thousand words.

~

Getting to Know Daddy

A heavy semester over
and Christmas break started.
Cherry hardly saw her daddy in four months.
They get to know each other again.

Stroll snowy Main Street; she snuggles in his arms.
We study the gingerbread houses in store windows.
Our favorites: Noah's Ark, Phantom of the Opera,
and a country store surrounded by popcorn-ball apple trees.

We hang glow-in-the-dark stars.
Daddy holds her up and
she tacks them to her ceiling.
"Twinkle Star." She grins at Daddy.

He takes off his glasses and, like the Invisible Man,
he looks one way and the glasses look another.
She tries to sneak up on him, but the glasses catch sight of her,
even when Daddy doesn't. She giggles and darts back.

Choo-choo-train rides on Daddy's back,
taking the long journey
around the couch, to Neverland, and back.
They decide an airplane is faster.
He swoops her through the air.

He sings "Row your boat" with her puppet dragon.
One time I join in, and Cherry covers my mouth,
as if to say "shsh, I'm listening."

Daddy and daughter leap around like frogs.
I kiss my prince,
but he remains a frog,
for his princess' daughter's sake.

~

Gravity

I climbed as soon as I could walk.
A scar across my forehead testifies
to my very first memory:
skydiving off the bunk bed.

My daughter inherited my sense of adventure.
I hope soon she'll learn that gravity exists,
and applies to her.

Until then I try to catch her—
as she dances on couch arms,

teeters on high edges,
and leaps from chair to chair.

⌇

Anatomy Art Lesson
Part I
Cherry's been drawing faces for months, with eyes, ears, mouth, nose, cheeks, and hair. I decided to introduce arms to her drawing. I'd heard that children draw "tadpole" people with the arms and legs coming off the face before they do the body, so I started showing her arms off the lower part of the face. She seemed really confused.

After a couple weeks I added an oval below the face and said stomach, then I added arms and legs off the stomach. Her face lit up as she repeated what I said. Then she called out *arm, hand, fingers, thumb, leg, toes* and even *knees* even before I drew them. A few days later, she drew her own people complete with stomachs, fingers, toes, and knees.

Silly Mom, don't you know arms don't grow on faces?

Part II
Cherry added eyebrows to her faces and pupils to the eyes. I pointed to an eyebrow and asked what it was. She shrugged her shoulders as if to say; *I don't know the name, but I see them on faces.*

⌇

Plank Drawings
Cherry walks her toes up the back of the chair until her ankles hang on the top and her elbows rest on the table. In the plank position of a yoga master, she draws.

INTO THE OVEN: ECZEMA

Just as the heat of the oven changes a pie from doughy shell and cold fruit to crispy crust and bubbling sweetness, the trials in life with God's blessings change me bit by bit, refining out my faults and brightening my strengths. These times help me become what I know I should be: patient, loving, forgiving, and faithful. And though the heat is painful, the raw ingredients become delicious through the baking.

Motherhood changed my body.
Hormones and hips shifted.
Sleep came in one- to two-hour snatches.
All normal and expected.

Eczema snuck in as a surprising thief.
My hands pocketed with pus.
I scratched in my sleep until they bled.
I tried different eczema creams—none helped.

Study and prayer, trial and error,
we found some of the triggers
–all lotions and hand sanitizers,

diaper wipes and most soaps,
sugar and stress.

I bought rubber gloves for dishwashing,
disposable gloves for diaper changing.
'Gratefuls' and walks helped with stress.
I tried to avoid sugar.

I itched less, but patches
continued to haunt me.

I was a mother, wife, tutor, and piano teacher.
Eczema was just one part of life.
As I'm strengthened by God's grace,
it has become a counterpoint to joyous living,
enriching life through the contrast.

Over the years, the eczema slowly disappeared. Now I only get it if I eat or touch something that my body reacts to, or if I'm under a lot of stress. I'm so grateful for both the knowledge of what to avoid and the blessing of healing.

SLICE 3: PECAN ENTERS AND SIBLING FUN

Nesting

Nesting shows up in different ways. Some expectant mothers paint the nursery or sew quilts. I write—capturing the beauty of reality and creating the excitement of fantasy.

Just as a child in the womb can hear her pianist mother play and grow to love music, will my children gain a love for story?

~

Butterflies

We're on the way to the hospital;
our son will be here soon.
I have butterflies in my stomach.

"What?" Jesse asks. "I thought you had a baby there."

I laugh.
Maybe I have both.
Will butterflies come out with this baby?

~

When Things Fall

I lay Pecan in his bassinet.
He's peacefully sleeping, grasping the blanket's edge.

As I stand, a rapid pounding thumps above,
Thump, thump,
Thump, thump, thump!

I scream, lunging for my baby.

A large something falls,
striking my hand,
shattering at my feet.

Clutching my baby, I flip on the light;
a bare bulb clings to the ceiling.

The heavy glass dome lies in shards at my feet,
scattered through the bassinet,
tinkling off the blanket,
falling from my pants.

Pecan is screaming. I am crying, searching him
for cuts.

He has none.

My knees are weak.
I fall to them in prayer.
"Thank Thee,
my baby is unhurt.
Thank Thee

for protecting us."

I'm still uncertain what caused the loud thumping or the light fixture to fall. But I know that Heavenly Father protected my infant, in part by giving me the warning of noise before the heavy glass dome fell into his bassinet.

$\approx$

Lightning Hands

Pecan has lightning-fast hands. I carry him on my hip and he grabs everything, even if it doesn't seem in reach. One day he grabbed a mixing bowl that had a chef's knife in it. Everything went into slow/fast motion, as I thought, *I'll catch it,* and moved to, then thought, *better not,* and stepped back to let the bowl and knife clatter to the floor.

$\approx$

Sibling letters

Letter from Cherry (age 2)

Dear Nana and Papa,

Guess what? I'm learning to count on my fingers. I say, "1, 2, 3, 5". Mommy keeps saying "4" in there, but I'm not quite sure where it goes yet.

Mommy bundled me up and I made lots of footprints in the snow. I want to play in it again, but it's all stomped down now and icy. I hope we get some more snow.

Daddy and I played some fun games. He took off his glasses and made them look at me while he looked at Mommy. Then his glasses looked at the book and then back at me. He's so funny. I giggled and giggled. We also played peek-a-boo with my stuffed animals.

Mommy and I bowled on the kitchen floor, knocking over plastic cups with a big ball. I ask her for Music and then I dance and dance.

When I ask for Movie, she usually puts on Music anyway, so I've stopped asking for Movie, most of the time.

Lots of love,
Cherry

Letter from Pecan (5 months old)

I discovered food, but no one will give it to me, except for rice cereal. I'm sure I can handle it. I got the spoon into my mouth (true, I gagged myself, but I'll learn). I tried to pry Cherry's fingers off her sippy cup and grab food off Mommy's plate. I get so hopeful when Mommy brings the spoon up, but then she eats it instead of giving it to me. It's so hard being a baby. In the meantime, I do like rice cereal.

Love,
Pecan

~

Sibling Opposites

She carefully unwraps a present, pulling tape away from the
    paper.
He tears the wrapping apart then stuffs it in his mouth.

She eats only certain foods. It is a red-letter day when she tries
    something new.
She likes strong flavors: seaweed paste, rye bread, broccoli,
    sweet and sour meatballs.
She despises oatmeal and willingly skips meals rather than
    eat it.

As I balance him on my hip, he grabs food from my hand,
a fist full of bread from a new loaf. He gags himself on a carrot.
I make chocolate-dipped strawberries
and he shoves one of my chocolate-coated fingers in his mouth.

She's content with a ten-word vocabulary,
using pantomime, pretend, and pulling me along to show her
    needs.
She draws people before she speaks more than two-word
    phrases.

He babbles from day one: coos, gurgles, cries,
watching us intently and taking turns,
as if he's carrying on a conversation.

Her vocabulary expands with her brother's.
Did he teach her to speak?

∾

Dressing Up – Two-Year-Old Version

Experiment One
Beautiful blue,
it has a dragon too.
Soft and snuggly.
It is just right for me.

Squeeze one arm through a sleeve.
Squeeze another arm through a leg.
Shoulders pull tight,
Arms locked behind.

Three-month-old clothes
Not fitting two-year-old.

"I'm stuck!"

Experiment Two
Red, pink, green, yellow,

stretchy, springy, oh so pretty.
Only two fit my hair.
How about my legs down there?

Pull one on, pull on twenty,
rainbow socks, colors aplenty.

Oh, oi! Pain and hurt!
Hair elastics on legs don't work!

~

The Bear and the Salad Tongs

I chop onions at the counter, preparing dinner.
A growling creeps closer, then ROAR!
A bear puppet hugs my leg.
Cherry laughs and runs off with the puppet.

Minutes later, she opens the kitchen drawer.
Click-clack-growl, she pinches my pants
between plastic salad tongs.

I set aside the onion and join the game;
tag around the kitchen table and the couch.
She the mighty salad-tong monster,
and I, her laughing prey.

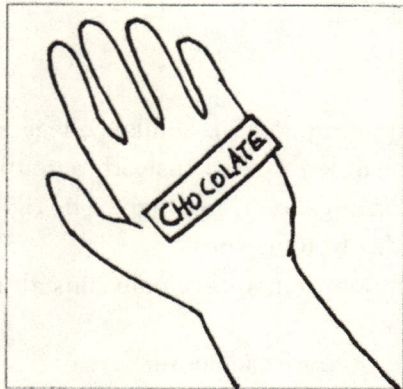

BAKER'S TIP: PARENTING 101

Parenting is hard. Unlike college, it doesn't come with a textbook and scheduled exams. Instead, parenting pop quizzes pounce like a tiger morning, noon, and night. The right answer yesterday may still be right today, or it may not.

Some answers remain constant:

- Love each other
- Love your children
- Be calm before correcting
- Counsel together as parents
- Trust God and seek His help
- Get up and try again

We're a three-way partnership, and the only Perfect One in the partnership makes up for all our mistakes, as long as we keep trying.

INTO THE OVEN: BATTLES AND MIRACLES

Sometimes it is another person going through the baking of a trial, but I feel the heat with them, and we both change.

Fasting and Prayer

A required class.
Four months' hard labor.
A project due.
Looming fear of failure.

Jesse worked on an engineering project all semester. He'd had one technical problem after another, ones that baffled even the lab assistant. Yet despite all his intense labor, if he didn't finish by the next day, he'd fail the class.

I didn't know what to do except fast, pray, and hope. As I prayed throughout the day, a feeling of peace wrapped around me. When Jesse got home that evening, he had figured out the last issue and the teacher had extended the due date by three days.

I'm so grateful for these blessings. Both that he finished the project and for the peace.

~

Miracles in the Burnout

From Journal Entries

Jesse is thirteen credits away from getting his bachelor's in Electrical Engineering and he's burnt out. After three long years of going full steam in a difficult engineering degree and working to provide for a family, he's hit his wall.

It's not just the work involved. He feels trapped in the Electrical Engineering major. He doesn't care for the environment at his summer internships and doesn't feel good about going into that same environment for full-time employment. But he feels he should still get his master's so he can be gainfully employed.

We study and pray, worry and pray, talk and pray.

Then we change the line of questioning from how to make this work, to what he enjoys doing. He brightens. He enjoys his student job at the Education Technology Center helping students, mentoring, and creating training modules.

We look at what major would lead to that sort of job and learn about the master's in Instructional Technology. It is only offered as a master's, and any bachelor's degree can apply. Jesse is excited about school again. It's been a while.

Now the hard part will be making it through the rest of this semester, then the last thirteen credits. He's still burnt out. He's going to talk to his professors and see what he needs to do to pass, because he's fallen behind. I pray that he may find the energy and motivation to finish these classes and his bachelor's degree. The worst-case scenario is that he fails one or several of these classes, loses his scholarship, and we have to take more time to finish his bachelor's degree in Electrical Engineering.

Surprisingly that doesn't produce the "end of the world" feeling I thought it would. We will make it through whatever comes. Heavenly

Father has watched over and blessed us countless times and continues to do so. I'm so grateful to God. I'm grateful for my husband who has worked and fought so hard these last three years, going to school, working, being a wonderful husband and father. I love him.

After note: He passed all his classes and kept his scholarship. We are truly blessed!

Scripture thought: Obedience—even when we don't know how it will work.

> But Jesus said unto them, They need not depart; give ye them to eat.
>
> And they say unto him, We have here but five loaves, and two fishes.
>
> He said, Bring them hither to me.
>
> And he commanded the multitude to sit down on the grass, and took the five loaves, and the two fishes, and looking up to heaven, he blessed, and brake, and gave the loaves to his disciples, and the disciples to the multitude.
>
> And they did all eat, and were filled: and they took up of the fragments that remained twelve baskets full. —Matthew 14:16-20

Jesus didn't ask the apostles to figure out how to do the miracle. He only asked them to give what they had, and then He made it enough. Sometimes it may feel as though we are asked to feed 5000 on little. But if we give our best effort, trusting in Him, He will make it enough.

~

Enough

"Is it enough to do my best,
even if it isn't perfect?"
Jesse's question shakes me.

He's already doing more
than I could ever do,
with the pressure of school, work,
and being a husband and father.

I hold him and whisper my love.
He is more than enough.
He's a wonder!

Oh, how I love him.

BAKER'S TIP: LESSONS IN THE FIRST FOUR YEARS OF MARRIAGE

"If someone needs an answer now, the answer is no. If they give us time to think about it, the answer may change."[1] We experienced the bitter lesson several times of saying yes to major changes, without taking the proper time to study it and pray together.

Forgive.

Communicate.

There is no problem too big to take to God in prayer.

Face challenges together as husband and wife. Trust each other and treat each other with respect.

We both have weaknesses. Help each other while being patient.

. . .

Tag-team in corrections. When one parent is at their wits' end, the other takes over. But whoever corrected also will be the one to comfort the child upon coming out of time-out, so the child feels that parent's love.

Our family thrives on consistency and stability.

Compliments and encouragement help. Criticism and nagging hurt.

I'm grateful for chances to change and to do better.

When we both were under extreme stress with school, work, and month-long house guests, someone said I should go away for several weeks with just our two children so my husband could learn to appreciate me. We didn't need to separate from each other; rather, we needed to re-prioritize about the situations that were straining our marriage and our family. We talked deeply about those situations, set up healthy boundaries, and put each other and our children first.

∼

Dates

Years of intense school, work, new babies, and internships
could wear out any relationship.

We work to strengthen ours with weekly dates,
where we set aside our worries
and see each other.

Push the couch to the edge of the room.
Dance party.

Read *Lord of the Rings*.
Three-year journey into Middle Earth,
intermixed with breaks into Lloyd Alexander.

Walks in the park.
Snowball fights.
Geeky jokes.
Snuggles.

Busy years, but not too busy for each other.

SLICE 4: CHILD SIGHT

Children see the world differently, with newness and excitement. They see what I've forgotten to notice, the common everyday things that are miracles and jokes and delights. Little by little, I learn to see with a childlike sight.

❧

After the Hug

When Jesse got home from work, Pecan ran and gave him a big hug and then cried for me. I took him, and then he cried for Daddy. So I came over and gave Daddy a big hug while holding Pecan.

Pecan turned Daddy's face towards mine, and my face towards Daddy's. He knew what came after a hug when Daddy comes home...a kiss!

❧

Auto Antics

Trick One
We drive through a puddle.

Our daughter squeals.
"The car is jumping in the puddles!"

Trick Two
Heavy dew coats the car.
Daddy wipes it off.
"Daddy mopped the car."

Trick Three
On Sunday:
"We're going to find the church."
And when we get home:
"You found our house."

Good old faithful car.

≈

Seasonal Negative

The black street and gray sidewalks are white
as if nighttime spilled paint.
The grass is a vibrant, summer green.

Fine snow sifted through grass blades.
Cold kept the snow-coated black top from melting.

"Mommy? Did someone shovel the lawn?"

≈

Cold

Half a week of severe weather.
So cold frost etches the

inside of our double-paned windows.
Low −15°F
High 0°F

We line the walls with quilts
Then snuggle with blankets,
mittens, hats, and hot chocolate.

Cherry begs, "Read the pig book."
We escape into *Charlotte's Web*.

∾

Starvation Walk

The weather warms.
My two littles bounce in the double stroller,
watching the world melt into spring.

Two miles later, we head for home.

Cherry protests, "No home! Walk!"
"We have to go home so we don't starve," I reason.
She tilts her head in thought. "I want to starve."

∾

Sharing

Pecan put a raisin in his mouth, took it out, and put it in Cherry's.

∾

Shadow Tag

Cherry played in a square of bright sunlight on the kitchen floor.
Daddy reached out his shadow and "caught" her feet and "tickled" her.

She jumped into the shadows, then cautiously stepped back into the patch of sunlight. Daddy's shadow crept towards her again. She laughed as she dodged his shadow tickles, then tried to catch the shadow monster.

∼

Cuteness Factor

Cherry said, "Mommy so cute. Baby Pecan so cute. Daddy so handsome. Cherry so silly."

~

BANG BANG BANG BANG BANG BANG BANG BANG BA
ANG BANG BANG BANG BANG BANG BANG

~

SLICE 5: PARENTING TWO—LAUGHTER AND LEARNING

Too Few Hands

Standing in line
at the county clerk's office.
Paperwork for a new-to-us car,
a babe in arms and toddler in tow.

The toddler, bored with waiting,
rips away from my grasp
into the hall.

I chase her all over the office building.
How is a child a quarter of my size so fast?

∿

Piano Lessons

Two of my piano students are siblings.

While I teach one, the other plays with my children,
building block castles to tumble under baby hands.

～

Thrift Store Run

We're moving apartments.
Don't need to bring everything with us.
The thrift store is just two blocks away,
and the weather is beautiful.
I'll just make a quick run.
Jesse has the car, but that doesn't matter;
the wagon will hold everything.

I pile the wagon,
strap my baby onto my back,
and set Cherry on the wagon's pile.

As we rumble along the sidewalk,
I glance at our shadows
shortened by the late morning sun.

I look like a child running away from home,
except I bring live dolls.

～

Potty Training

I've tried everything I can think of, all the tricks others have told
me, and nothing yet works, even after a year of trying. I pray about it
constantly.

The answer seems to be, "keep trying".

I know that I'm growing as a mother in patience and love. I know that my prayers have increased in sincerity and intent. As I've prayed for patience and charity, I've felt God's gift and blessings in these areas. "All things shall give you experience," and this, mundane as it is, is teaching me and stretching me.

~

SLICE 6: JOYOUS WELCOME AND PARENTING THREE

Thanksgiving Fun

Course 1—The Kitchen Dance

One pace wide,
two paces long,
a kitchen made for one.

Four friends weave through the space,
spilling into the living room.
A dish of green bean almondine
sashays by a pot of mashed potatoes.

Pans square dance
around burners,
simmer, boil, set to cool.

Roasting stuffing adds rich low notes
to the high sweet notes of cooling pies.
Laughter punctuates the aromatic orchestra.

Course 2 – Thankfuls

Stomachs over full,
laughter overflowing.
Family encircling the table.

Parents, siblings, cousins, aunts and uncles,
husband, two children.
A circle of love.

We take turns saying a "thankful".
School, family, memory.
My turn: "My three children."

Confused silence turns into cheers.

Course 3 – Games

Apples to Apples
The Renaissance:
Venice, Sistine chapel,
Leonardo—he was the Renaissance!

Who, What, Where
What does Jack Frost eat?
Bike tires, walnut shells,
everyone's left shoe.

Fork and Spoon
This is a fork.
A what?
A fork—a spoon!
What!!?

We laugh so hard we
turn red for lack of breath.

Course 4 – The Competition

A balloon floats near by,
its string four feet from the ground.
Who can capture it?
No hands allowed.

My brother leaps and tries to
catch the string between his feet.

The other men join in,
heaving feast-laden bodies into acrobatics.
The balloon evades them.

I balance on one foot and
capture the string
between my toes.

∿

Locked out

An easy three-hour labor,
and a baby who sleeps in four-hour stretches.
I'm feeling great
four days into motherhood of three.

I doze in the August sun on our apartment patio
while my baby naps and my other two play with blocks.
Everyone said three is the hardest transition,
but this is no harder than two.

Then my two-year-old cries at the patio door.
The door is locked, deadbolted,
and my three children are inside without me.

"Pecan, open the door."
He tries and cries harder.
Cherry is gone, where?
I yell through the door,
"Cherry! Please help."

A minute plods by to the
wailing of my two-year-old.

I'm on the second floor.
No neighbors are around.
Should I climb over the railing
and leap to the grass?
Probably not the best postpartum exercise.
I swing my leg onto the railing.

Cherry comes to the door.
"Mommy, baby Apple is crying."

"Cherry, please unlock the door."

She does.

I gather my sobbing two-year-old
and hungry infant
into my arms.
Cherry goes back to drawing.

I spoke too soon.
Three will be a learning experience.

~

Toy Squabbles

She has a toy.
He grabs it.
She hits.
He cries.
She goes into time-out.
We talk about gentleness.
Repeat.

Time to change the cycle.
Prayer and planning.
Practice with children.
We'll see what happens.

She has a toy.
He grabs it.
She offers him a different toy.
He still takes her toy.
She hits.
He cries.
I put the toy up high.
"The toy needs a time-out."
She watches, eyes wide.

Days later, the toy comes down.
She takes it with a promise:
"I won't hit anymore.
I don't like my toy in time-out."

She has a toy.
He grabs it.

She offers him a different toy.
He still takes her toy.
She calls for help.
I remove him.
She gets to keep her toy.

I discovered that she didn't mind being in time-out. She liked to sit quietly and have a place to think. But she didn't like her toy being in time-out. Over time the toys spent less and less time in time-out, while my children learned to get along better.

≈

Slept Well Several Times

Apple has started waking up every couple of hours through the night until 3 a.m., when she finally sleeps until morning. Now Pecan has started to wake up at 4 a.m., and though he goes back to sleep, I'm up at 6 a.m. to start the day. I don't think I've had more than two hours of sleep in a row for the last week, or as my dad once said, "I've slept well several times."

This makes me grateful for the many months that Apple slept well and through the night. I hope this waking up every two hours is a short phase, but I survived it with Cherry for a whole year, so I know it is possible.

Two weeks later: Apple's sleeping through the night, as are all the other children! I'm feeling much more energetic. I'm enjoying it while it lasts, and I'm so grateful for it.

≈

First Chapter Books

Charlotte's Web
Pippi Longstocking

Little House in the Big Woods
Fablehaven
Pollyanna

They play while I read. I wonder if they listen, but each time I close the book they plead for more.

~

SLICE 7: CHILDHOOD WISDOM

First Poetry

Not quite two years old, Pecan made his first poetry. He sneezed then said, "achoo, bless you, tissue."

~

Moddy

Pecan would sometimes start to ask me for something and then realize I wasn't at the table, so he would change to asking Daddy. The result was "Moddy" (Mommy/Daddy).

~

Imagination

Seeing One

My oldest brings an
invisible cluster of balloons to the car.
She holds the string tightly in her hand

then gives one to Pecan, Daddy, and me.

As I get into the car, she says,
"Mommy, your balloon popped."

Seeing Two

Cherry's eyes widen as
we watch lightning flash
in a summer storm.

"Oh no, the clouds are broken!
How did the lightning do that?"

Seeing Three

"Where's my toothbrush?"

Cherry looks up from drawing.
"The dragon ate it."

Seeing Four

I slice the cucumber.
Cherry watches.
"Poor cucumber; he's crying!"
She points to the tear-shaped seeds,
then eats a slice.

~

Relationship Lingo

Cherry was trying to figure out family relationships and their titles.
She said to me, "Daddy is your father?"
"Daddy is your daddy, but he's my husband."

She said, "Jane is my husband."

I was very confused at first then realized she was talking about her cousin Jane. "Jane is your cousin."

"Oh, my cousin!"

Two Months later:

Cherry explained to Pecan, "Grandpa Joe is Daddy's Mommy's husband."

~

Surprise Dessert

Peach sorbet for dessert.
Cherry left a melted puddle
in the bottom of her bowl.

Never one to let
good food go to waste,
I tip the bowl to drink it.

Jesse asks Cherry,
"Why didn't you eat it all?"

She replies, "It's drool."

~

Noise

Pecan fills his days with noise:
laughter, shouts, loud monologues.

Cherry is usually a bubble of quiet

drawing, thinking, looking at books.

Their worlds collide in a small apartment.
I advise Cherry, "Cover your ears."

"Mommy, I'm covering his ears,
and I can still hear him!"

∾

When Daddy Comes Home

Cherry usually didn't wake up before Jesse left in the morning, and she was asleep before he got home at 10 p.m. on Tuesdays. So when he came home one Wednesday evening just before bedtime, she said, "Daddy, you came back tonight!"

∾

Apple the Bear

She started to growl at us one spring. We thought it was so cute that we laughed and growled back. All things reinforced continued. For the next year Apple had a very deep growl, like a little bear, to counterpart her high happy squeals.

∾

What an Apple Is

Apple ran around in only her diaper.
Jesse greeted her, "Hi, Bare."
"I'm not a bear!"
"Are you a cat?"
She shook her head with a big grin. "No."
"Are you silly?"
"No!"

"Who are you?"
"Um... a girl!"

~

Chocolate Chili

I made chocolate chili. Cherry said, after she tasted it, "Mommy, chocolate chips go in cookies, not chili."

~

Daddy

Pecan was calling me "Daddy" so I asked him, "Who am I?"
He replied, "You're Daddy, Mommy!"

~

Atlantis

Cherry asked for some "Atlantis" while pointing to the enchiladas.
Jesse said, "Atlantis is a city."
"It's not a city, it's like a grasshopper."
"Oh, you mean a preying mantis."
"Yes, a praying mantis."
"Are you sure you want to eat a preying mantis, or would you like some enchiladas?"
"Yes, enchiladas."

~

SLICE 8: WHEN I WAS A PIE
AND OTHER CONVERSATIONS WITH PECAN

When I Was a Pie

"The last time you flew,"
Papa says, "Cherry was a toddler,
and Pecan was in the oven."
Referring to my pregnancy.

Nana shakes her head.
"Be careful with that term.
Pecan is literal."

Ten minutes later
Pecan declares,
"When I was a pie,
I was in the oven."

~

Fly Bait
Pecan saw a fly and tried to swat it with the fly swatter. Nana

suggested setting out a piece of food to attract it. A minute later Pecan was marching around with the fly swatter in one hand and a piece of candy in the other hand, saying "Here, fly, come here, fly."

∾

Pushing Buttons

I asked Pecan,
"What should you do if I say 'no'?"

"I should growl
and tickle your button."

∾

Dialog #1
"I like colds," said Pecan.
I raised my eyebrows. "A cold is when you cough and your throat hurts."
"I don't like colds; I like warms."

∾

Dialog #2
Pecan said, "I want to fly to Grandmama's house."
I replied, "Flying takes lots of money. Daddy has to earn the money."
"I'm going to be a flyer dragon and fly to Grandmama's house then turn into a human. Then it won't take money."

∾

Dialog #3

We were helping with digging out a fruit room at my parents'. After a long day of work, my brother lay down on the lawn to nap.

Pecan walked up to him.

Bob asked, "What are you doing?"

"Going to sit on your lap."

"But I don't want you to sit on my lap. I'm sleeping."

"We don't sleep outside. We sleep inside," Pecan said.

"I'm going to sleep outside. You sleep inside. I'm dirty."

Pecan studied him. "You're dirty. We need to clean you off. We need water. Where's the hose?"

SLICE 9: DOUBLE MAJORS

Cruse of Oil

We wanted to climb our education mountain, without digging a hole of debt.

We took out our first student loan for the last year of Jesse's graduate school, and paid the loan off within six months of him getting a full-time job.

It was a worked-for, prayed-for, and blessed miracle.

Jesse worked 20-hour weeks every semester and full time in the summer, saving everything possible for next year's tuition. He worked just as hard for a high GPA so he could keep his scholarships.

I worked at a call center and as an office assistant before we had children. And after children, I babysat, taught piano, and tutored.

We stretched our student income over rent, food, transportation, and the occasional doctor's visit. We furnished our apartment and ourselves with thrift store treasures.

And through it all we always had enough.

I know that God blessed us as we obeyed his law of tithes and offerings. We gave that small part back of what He gave us, and He made the remainder last like the cruse of oil and the handful of meal (1 Kings 17:10-16).

~

Caught Moments

Time together doesn't just happen.
He's gone at classes and work.
I'm mothering three children.

So we catch moments,
pulling toward each other,
even as the days pull us apart.

When kids are asleep,
before they wake.
Whispered conversations,
muffled laughs.

Studying together.
Reading dry engineering books
and brainstorming projects.

Getting a babysitter
for time at the temple.
Finding peace in service.

A walk to the park.
While kids play,
we share our separate days,
merging them into one.

Giggles over dinner-time jokes,
while trying to get kids to eat.

Caught moments.
Pulling together.

Binding our hearts
with time-captured love.

～

Double Majors

Marriage is so much more than sharing a home and each taking a portion of the chores. It is bearing with each other's burdens, cheering each other's goals, moving forward together toward God.

While in school we had the unique opportunity to support each other. My husband has an artist's touch but majored in Electrical Engineering and Instructional Technology to better provide for our family. I have a talent for math and science, but majored in my love of writing. My husband also has dyslexia—the words crawl across the page like ants when he's tired.

He supported me in my writing and music classes by providing insight and clarity to my ideas.

I supported him in his engineering, math, and science classes by brainstorming on assignments and reading his texts out loud when he grew so tired that the words swam.

We unofficially double majored. We are engineering artists and artistic instructors.

INTO THE OVEN: THE JOB SEARCH

Some bake times are quick and hot while others are long and low. This job search was a long, long baking time, slowly changing us in a way that a quick, hot trial could not have.

Job Hunt

Ten long months,
hunting a full-time job.
He has his masters degree.
He's applying
and interviewing.
We're praying and hoping.

Hopes rise with
follow-up interviews
and crash with
"You are highly qualified,
but we decided to not
fill the position at this time."

The economy is in a downturn.

He takes on temp jobs:
painting, office work,
and continues to
drive to distant interviews,
make samples of his work,
and pray.

The repeated emotional
climbs and falls
wrench our hearts.

I've never liked
roller coasters.
But I love my ride-mate,
and we'll finish this ride
together.

~

Lessons Learned in the Job Search

The year of unemployment was the hardest year of our marriage. Jesse worked harder than anyone I know through our years of school—going to school full time and supporting a family. But as the months after graduation passed and all his efforts to get a full-time job continued to fall through, he retreated from the discouragement into distractions. As he neared the 10-month mark of being out of work, he was spending more time on video games than job searching. We were down to our last $4. My tutoring was our main income.

We talked and prayed and had two strong impressions:

- "When you learn how to work, I will give you employment."
- "It doesn't matter if you are bringing in an income, but you must be working."

After we counseled together, Jesse packed up all his video games. Neither of us slept that night. Serious discussion and resultant revelation kept us in thinking insomnia.

At 2 a.m. Jesse rolled over. "I'm sorry."

I embraced him. "I love you. We'll get through this."

The next morning, Jesse headed out the door to paint a house. He'd done many temp jobs over the year, but he promised to be out doing something to help someone for a full work day, every day, then job search in the evening.

When he got home that evening, he opened his email to apply for jobs and found a job offer!

I broke down in tears. I didn't expect the answer to come so quickly. We suffered through a year of unknown and learned some important lessons. Those lessons have blessed us in subsequent years.

Lessons Learned:

- Initiative: Don't wait for someone to give an assignment. See a need and fill it. Be actively engaged in a good cause.
- Patience: Patience isn't idly waiting for things to happen—but doing all we can while trusting God to make up for what we have no control over, and trusting His timing. Fret not but have faith.
- Increased love and compassion: We both increased in love and compassion as we struggled side by side. We learned even as there were many things we had no control over, we do have control of how we treat each other and our children.
- Lovingly take a stand: When Jesse fell into depression under the weight of repeated rejections, I didn't want to add to his burden. But we needed to talk, and we needed to take action. We counseled together. It was a tear-wrenching discussion. He knew he needed to get up and go again, but it took counseling together to break the stasis.
- Gratitude: See with gratitude. Live with gratitude.

And Especially Faith:

We knew that the Lord loved us. We knew that it was a righteous desire of my husband to work and provide for our family. We were trying to keep the commandment to labor for our living. We trusted that the Lord would provide a way to accomplish that command.

> I will go and do the things which the Lord hath commanded, for I know that the Lord giveth no commandments unto the children of men, save he shall prepare a way for them that they may accomplish the thing which he commandeth them.
> –1 Nephi 3:7

But months passed. It became hard to keep trying. Jesse had worked hard to gain his degree, and I'd assumed that he'd get a full-time job within a month or so. That assumption led to discouragement when the desired employment didn't happen.

That year humbled me. I learned to wait upon our Lord (Isaiah 40:31). He granted us peace and guidance, but not the desired answer, for almost a year. We needed that year to grow as individuals, as a couple, and as followers of Christ.

Perhaps most of all, I learned to have faith in God and not the answer.

> I had desired to know the things that my father had seen, and believing that the Lord was able to make them known unto me...
> – 1 Nephi 11:1

Nephi said he knows God "was able" to show him, not that he knows He "will" show him. Nephi's faith was in God and His omnipotence, love and goodness, not faith that Nephi's will would be done. "I desire" instead of "I demand".

I grew from expectation of blessings, to distress and discouragement, to trust and hope—not in the circumstance but in our Lord who was watching over us.

SLICE 10: TENDER MERCIES

Angel at the Gas Station

A 750-mile drive.
Three kids.
Intense carsickness.

Gas station clean up.
Our infant screams,
toddler sits stunned,
oldest retches again.
Car fills with acid fumes.

I scrape vomit from upholstery.

A man hands us a folded check.
"God bless you" and is gone.

An angel sent to let us know
God sees our struggles and loves us.

~

Valentines

Crayons and markers scatter
higgledy-piggledy across the table.
Bits of red and pink float to
join the paper-drift below the chairs.

Cherry draws a purple mermaid on a red heart.
"I want to make a valentine
for the people who don't have houses."
She adds roses, smiley faces, and hearts.

We send them to the homeless shelter,
grateful that even though
Daddy doesn't have a job yet,
we do have a home.

~

Magic

We look at a Scripture picture book
"God created the
mountains and streams,
plants and animals."

Cherry touches the pictures.
"Heavenly Father knows
how to use magic!"

I snuggle her closer.
"His power is even

stronger than magic.
He made everything,
because He loves you."

BAKER'S TIP: PARENTING 201

PARENTING CONFESSIONS FROM A MOTHER OF THREE

I usually write about the fun and good things. But our kids have their share of yelling, hitting, meltdowns, stubbornness, and messes. And as parents, we sometimes lose our tempers, give projects and things priority over kids, and aren't very good examples. I just don't like writing about those times. So if I give the mistaken impression that I have perfect children and we are perfect parents, we are not. We are struggling parents trying to do our best, and we are so grateful for the atonement and for children who love us even when we make so many mistakes.

That being said, a cousin asked for parenting advice. So here's my ten cents (a long ten cents).

First: You have and will get lots of advice from all sources. Much of what I do as a parent, I've learned from my parents, family and friends. I'm so grateful to them. But the best piece of advice I received is: trust God and yourself, and if the advice doesn't fit with these two, then don't fret about it. What works for my family may not work for yours. Find what does.

Second: Pray and study things out. Pray and keep praying for charity, patience and any attribute you are trying to develop and strengthen. Once you are done praying, study this attribute. I love the Scriptures,

General Conference[1], and the Ensign[2]. I find Heavenly Father most often gives me needed answers through these sources. Keep close to the Holy Ghost. Find a quiet time to pray and study. It helps.

Third: There are some resources for universal parenting advice. "The Family: A proclamation to the World" is one. Doctrine and Covenants 121:41-46 is another. Study these.

Ideas that Work for Us:

1. Never discipline in anger. And always follow up with love. Time-outs give me time to cool down as well.

2. Ask, Practice, and Praise: for Bad Behavior

- Ask: Make sure the child understands what is wrong, and suggest a good behavior to replace it.
- Practice the good behavior three times (or however many times you feel is good)
- Praise each time for the good behavior (even though it is just a practice)

3. Ask, Practice, and Praise: for Good Behavior

- Do the same for any good behavior you are trying to develop. This works great for me: practice what I'm going to do as a parent (instead of just thinking about it)—going through the motions helps it stick.

4. Praise instead of criticize. Focus on the good. Build others up. Follow correction with love.

5. Have the same rules for everyone in the house (children and parents). For example: if I expect the kids to respond when I say their names, then I need to respond to them as quickly.

6. Keep it simple. Have clear, simple expectations or family rules. When someone does something wrong, ask, "what should you do instead?" Usually they know, and if they don't, then it is a great time to teach. And if they continue not to understand, then it is probably time to simplify the rule.

7. Take time to laugh and play with your kids in one form or another. I love to read to them, but I'm not so good at playing with them. Jesse is really good at playing with them and being silly. The kids love both. Do things that you enjoy and they enjoy too.

8. Listen, listen, listen. I'm really working on this one.

∾

Responsibility

Cherry and Pecan painted
Grandmama's walls with her makeup.
They helped clean it up,
then took on another chore
for the mess and waste.

I worked beside Cherry weeding the garden.

She gave every excuse:
"I'm tired.
I'm sick.
I'm really sick; I need medicine.
I'm concerned.
I'm scared; I don't like spiders.
I'm disappointed."

I listened,
didn't say much,
and kept working,
taking her hands in mine,
and pulled weeds.

Complaints died to
quiet work.
Cherry's proud smile
lit the end.

PIE AFTER COLLEGE

Jesse started work. We found an apartment and a little later bought our first house. We welcomed our fourth child, Lime. College had ended, but not learning. Never that.

SLICE 1: LIME ARRIVES

Our fourth child came when we were between our student insurance and Jesse's work insurance. We found a wonderful midwife and he was born at home. He came with a quiet, curious personality and a bright smile.

Thinking Outside the Toy Box

Lime thinks outside the box, the toy box, that is. He can be surrounded by his toys but goes for the things that we keep taking away from him. He is our first child to put everything in his mouth and he is always after the shoes, electrical cords, outlets, and Lego. He's fast and persistent! We tucked the refrigerator cord behind it, and he keeps fishing it back out.

INTO THE OVEN: WAITING ON THE LORD

I thought Jesse's year of job searching was difficult. And it was. This time the extended trial was vastly different. Whereas Jesse could do something about seeking a job, the following experience truly taught us to wait upon the Lord.

Answered Prayer

This experience prepared me for what came next.

Mother of four,
teething baby,
little sleep.

Kids being kids,
the noise mounts,
my nerves unravel.
I ask with frustration,
"What should I do,
when you don't listen?"

My five-year-old teaches:

"Pray that we will listen."

Humbled, I pray, "Please,
change *my* heart,
to peace and charity,
despite what happens."

The next day
fills with as much
noise and busy mothering,
yet peace and calm surround me,
buffering the storm.
I see clearly what is
important and what to let slide.

Two days of grace.
Then the washer breaks,
flooding the house.
My husband injures his back.
Yet the blessing of peace
remains in force.

I don't know how long I'll
have this peace and calm.
Longer if I heed the promptings.

I'm ashamed to admit,
sometimes I ignore the buffer to think
and instead choose to be angry.

But I'm learning,
I'm changing,
through the grace of God.

❧

Waiting on the Lord

Around nine months old, our fourth child, Lime, developed eczema: an oozing itch that he scratched at until it bled. We went to doctors, tried creams, and cut all variety from his diet. We pled in prayer and sought direction in the temple. We held him, loved him, and cried for him. But nothing we did seemed to make a difference, and the problem only grew worse for many months.

The many priesthood blessings were hard and wonderful. Each time, Heavenly Father told us He was aware of our baby's trial and that eventually he'd be restored to full health. He blessed our baby to be comforted. He blessed us to be at peace in our hearts. He blessed each of us to learn what we needed to through this time. He told us that this would continue until we learned the things we needed to learn.

I prayed that I would quickly learn what I needed to learn so my child would not have to suffer any more.

I learned what it means to wait upon the Lord. It requires complete trust in God, to keep going in what I can do and not lose hope, to acknowledge I cannot do it myself, to ask what the Lord wants me to do, then to follow the received direction even if it doesn't seem to make a difference, and to endure with gratitude. I learned to constantly seek direction and to be grateful for revelation as it came, step by step. Many times, I felt an overwhelming love and peace as I poured out my soul in prayer.

My faith and trust in God brought me closer to Him, opening my ears to hear what He wanted me to do—and usually that involved serving others. His blessing of peace and love showed me how to extend that same love and calmness to others. He taught me perspective and granted me strength to let go of those less important things, so I could attend to those most important: God, family, and neighbor.

After eight months brimful of tears and blessings, Heavenly Father sent us another blessing. Little by little, He took away the eczema.

～

Lessons Learned

Faith in God and Not the Miracle

> And, behold, there came a leper and worshipped him, saying, Lord, if
> thou wilt, thou canst make me clean.
> And Jesus put forth his hand, and touched him, saying, I will; be
> thou clean. And immediately his leprosy was cleansed.
> —Matthew 8:2-3

The leper said, "Lord, if *thou* wilt, thou canst make me clean." His
faith was founded in the Savior, not the miracle. We can learn so much
from his simple statement.

When we place our faith in the miracle or desire—*if I focus enough,
believe enough, have enough faith, this desired thing will happen*—then we
are building on a sandy foundation. In a sense, we are practicing idola-
try, because we're putting our faith in what we want instead of our faith
in God.

But when we place our faith in our Savior and His power and
wisdom, trusting that He loves us and will do what is best for us, then
we can ask in faith for what we desire, and work for it, all the while
trusting Him whether our desire is fulfilled or not. When the storms
and disappointments and trials of life come, we are founded on Him,
on the firm rock that will not fall.

Line upon Line

> For precept must be upon precept, precept upon precept; line upon
> line, line upon line; here a little, and there little:
> —Isaiah 28:10

Lime's severe eczema was mostly tied to food sensitivities. We did a
lot of trial and error to see what we could feed him. Though God was

helping us in the trial, He didn't give us all the answers. He guided us in our research, in finding certain doctors, in trying certain things. But it still was hard to see my baby scratching himself until he bled.

The story of Nephi and his brothers going to get the Scriptures strengthened me (see 1 Nephi 3 and 4).

"Nephi and his brothers tried three different times before they obtained the brass plates and in the process lost all their riches. Heavenly Father was guiding them, and each try was a step towards fulfilling the commandment. I need to keep hope and faithfully keep trying, keep seeking revelation, keep being thankful for each blessing along the way." - journal entry from the time when we still didn't know how to help our son.

Seek Daily Guidance

And we did follow the directions of the ball, which led us in the more fertile parts of the wilderness.
— 1 Nephi 16:16

God gave Lehi's family a physical tool, like a compass, to follow through the wilderness. But they had to look at it each day for direction.

"Going west yesterday doesn't mean going west today. In my life and for my son's health, I also need to daily check on what to do. The gospel is always sure, but the things that God doesn't reveal through Scripture leave me with the need to daily check back in with Him." - journal entry from the time when we still didn't know how to help our son.

Answered Prayers in God's Time

Yea, I know that God will give liberally to him that asketh. Yea, my God will give me, if I ask not amiss; therefore I will lift up my voice unto thee; yea, I will cry unto thee, my God, the rock of my righteousness.

Behold, my voice shall forever ascend up unto thee, my rock and mine everlasting God.

—2 Nephi 4:35

"Am I asking amiss for my son to be healed of his eczema? No. But to put it in a time frame, perhaps so. I am in a tutorial of patience and trusting in God's time frame. To trust Heavenly Father even with all the setbacks and unexplained flair-ups." - journal entry from the time when we still didn't know how to help our son.

Record Impressions

Heavenly Father helps me in my frailties even as Satan does his utmost to make me doubt spiritual impressions. As I receive impressions and direction on what to do, and also feelings about what is right, I record them in my journal. Then when doubts come—and they do—I'm able to go read and remember.

SLICE 2: ADVENTURES OF LIFE

Art Adventure

Opening night for the
International Children's Art Exhibit
with one of Cherry's paintings.

Daddy and I take her
to dinner at the Spaghetti Factory.
Then he drops us off
for the opening ceremonies.

He'll meet us in an hour
when he's picked up his
college-bound siblings
from the airport.

But he doesn't.

He calls.

Car accident.
No one's hurt.
He'll come ASAP.

I don't tell Cherry, yet.
This is her night.
We look at every painting.
She plays in the children's exhibit:
gardening, building, dancing.

The museum closes at 9 p.m.
I finally tell her, "Daddy's car got hurt,
but he's fine. He'll come soon."

She's disappointed he couldn't come,
but happy he's not hurt.
We'll wait for him in the
hotel lobby across the street.

Before we leave, a museum staff member
hands her four balloons
and wishes us luck.

Cherry sees a little girl crying
and gives her one of the balloons.

I hug her.
"You are so kind.
You gave away your
favorite color balloon."

She shrugs. "I think she likes pink too.
I only wanted three balloons anyway,
one for Pecan, Apple, and me."

9:50 p.m.
Daddy arrives with his two siblings,
and a car with a gaping hole
in the passenger side.

I send another prayer of thanks that
the person that hit them
only injured the car.

We head home,
our art adventure
inked in our memories.

~

Auto Blessings

One car, one family of six.
Ignition breaks.

No car, one family of six,
with job, shopping, and church.
No buses. We live in the middle of fields.

Bike to work—six miles uphill.
Coming home is a breeze.

Five miles to the closest store.
We enjoy food storage.

Church only half a mile away.
Engage double stroller and legs.
Kids sit tired and quiet in church.

A week of no car
and many blessings.

≈

County Fair

We wander the county fair, looking at Cherry's art, farm produce, 4H projects, and pigs. Our favorite spot is the children's science tent. Cherry and Pecan make ramps and race marbles.

Apple, age three, grabs my hand. "I want to see the spider." She leads me to a table with a live tarantula. She watches other kids hold the tarantula and then asks, "Can I hold the spider?"

She spreads out her hands.

The spider handler sets the tarantula gently in her hands. Its legs span larger than her two hands together.

It moves a leg.

Apple's eyes grow wide and her mouth opens in a large *O*. She hands it back and tells me with a tremor, "I didn't know it was alive."

≈

Christmas Interest

We stroll through the bright lights and loud music of the mall to see Santa. The kids cluster, in foot-tripping closeness. Cherry asks Santa for a nativity scene, Pecan asks for stickers, while Apple shyly waves.

Then we go to the garden center to pick out a Christmas tree. The kids scatter in all directions; running around the trees, jumping and looking. When we get them gathered again, I ask, "Why did you stay with us at the mall but scatter here?"

Cherry replies, "Because here is so much more interesting than the mall."

≈

Christmas Eve Haiku

> Ev'ry Christmas Eve
> I gather my kids to hear
> woven tales, magic.

> My oldest daughter
> takes the book. "I'll read to them."
> I slip out to wrap.

> Her words follow me:
> "Once upon a time, there was…"
> Old tales in new voice.

~

Children-Created Date

"Don't look!" Cherry shuts the door of the girls' bedroom. Giggles are muffled on the other side.

Apple slips out and dances by me, followed by Pecan. "Mommy, I can't wait to show you. It's—"

Pecan covers her mouth. "Don't tell her! Wait till tonight."

Friday evening comes. Our children drag Jesse and me to the girls' bedroom. I hold my toddler on my hip.

"Close your eyes," Cherry says.

The door swings open and we stumble blindly in, tugged by little hands.

"Surprise!" they yell.

We are in an explosion of dried flowers and ribbons. The kids' wicker table and chairs sit in the middle, set with toy dishes brimful of nuts, fruit, chocolates and other treats—from the kids' Christmas stockings two weeks before.

Cherry flips on a colored lamp while Pecan turns off the overhead light. Apple hands us a gift box, tied shut with a ribbon. Inside are three quarters, one from each of them, and a toy ring.

Then the three slip out with Lime toddling after them and watch a movie while we enjoy the sweet child-made date.

⁓

Prompting

I'm quite pregnant with child number five, and resting while the kids play in the backyard. I get a feeling that I should look for Lime. I step onto the deck and can't see him.

"Cherry, where is Lime?"

She stops swinging in the tree and looks around the side of the house, then takes off running as she calls back, "He opened the gate."

I run through the house and out the front door. We live on a busy street with semi-trucks that barrel by at 45 mph. Lime is almost to the end of the driveway as I dash down the front steps. Cherry flies across the driveway, her nine-year-old legs faster than my pregnant weighted ones. She catches his hand as he reaches the road.

I'm so grateful for the Holy Ghost's promptings and Cherry's speed to catch Lime. I learned again to never delay acting on a prompting. We now have a lock on the gate.

⁓

The Summer of Les Miserables

Cherry heard the story of the bishop who helped Valjean and wanted to read the rest of the story. She was only nine years old, so I started reading it out loud as an experiment to see if she and her younger siblings would understand and enjoy it. I chose the 600-page abridged version instead of the 1400-page version. They became engrossed in the story and wanted me to continue. So we spent the summer reading and discussing Jean Valjean and his epic journey. We especially talked about:

- Bravery, honor and helping people even when they are our enemies (Jean Valjean helping Javert and Marius).

- That Javert never really thought, but blindly followed, and that having to confront two "irreconcilable" choices destroyed him. But Jean Valjean was always thinking and weighing both sides and making choices based on his in-depth analyses (both mental and moral).

I'm grateful for the chance to learn beside my children, and for beautiful, deep thoughts embedded in a rich world of literature.

SLICE 3: IMAGINATION

Cherry Sweet

#I

Cherry drew a picture of Apple in a dress with squiggly lines all over it. She explained, "Those are worms because Apple is as cute as a bug."

#2

Jesse was playing frisbee with Pecan one evening, and Apple was outside too. Cherry came upstairs and asked, "Why are things so quiet?" The house was really quiet. I laughed at the realization of where the usual noise comes from.

#3

Before Lime got his tonsils out, he breathed loudly, especially when he slept. In the middle of one night Cherry had a nightmare and came upstairs. When she heard Lime's breathing she thought a wild animal was hiding in the hallway. She crashed into our room, crying, "There's a wolf or something in our house!"

~

Pecan's Wit

#*1*

"Guess what, Pecan? Your middle name is Daddy's name."
He turned to his sister. "My name is Pecan Daddy Farb."

#*2*

"Let's paint the garage, because it will kill the bugs, because paint is poisonous."

#*3*

Pecan said, "I'm a fire ghost," and sat on Cherry.
Cherry groaned and said, "Oh, why does the fire ghost have to be so heavy?"

#*4*

Pecan held a blanket wrapped into a bundle. "My baby is in here." He unwrapped it and held up a stuffed animal frog and dog. "The frog is my baby and the dog is his chew toy."

#*5*

Pecan saw his aunt in a ball gown. He said, "Your dress is beautiful because you are wearing it."

. . .

#6

Pecan wrote a couple notes to Santa. In one he said, "Dear Santa, I like to be silly." And in another he said, "Dear Santa, My favorite part of Christmas is the Nativity. Do you like the Nativity, too? Write yes or no below." And he drew a line for Santa to write on.

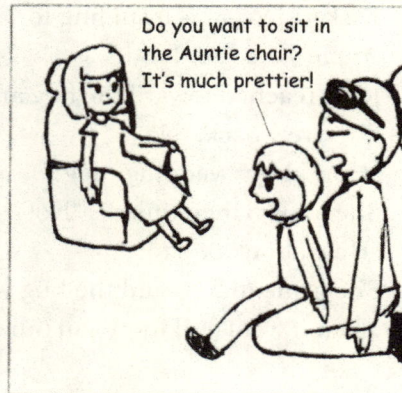

~

Joyful Conversations

#*I*

Nana: "Where are my shoes?"
Apple: "I ate them."
"Really?"
"Yes."
"Were they good?"
"Yum!"

#*2*

Apple said, "I'm a spider, a princess spider. Cherry is a bug. And Pecan is a prince."

#*3*

Apple was playing with a stuffed animal bug. She had it sniffing around the room.

I asked, "What is it sniffing for?"

Apple said, "For food."

Jesse reached toward the bug and said, "Here's a cupcake."

She drew back. "No."

"How about wedding cake?"

She looked incredulous. "No!"

"How about a carrot?"

She came to him and the bug went, "Yum, yum, yum," and ate it all up. Then it went and found an (imaginary) apple.

#*4*

On her fourth birthday, we asked Apple how old she was. She said three—when asked further, she said, "I'm not four until I eat my cake!"

~

Our Pet—the Dinosaur

Apple received a dinosaur egg in her Christmas stocking. It was a little larger than a chicken egg with the instruction to put it in water and watch it hatch over the next many days. About four days later the dinosaur was halfway hatched and Pecan asked, "What kind of food does Apple's dinosaur eat?"

I replied, "Plants."

"So it has armor to protect it from the T-rexes?"

"Yes."

"There's not many dinosaurs around here, are there?"

"Not any more."

"Except for ours."

I started laughing as I realized that Pecan thought Apple had a real dinosaur that we were hatching for a pet. "Pecan, Apple's dinosaur is a toy."

Pecan looked puzzled. "Oh, I thought it was alive—that we had a new pet. How did it get in the egg?"

～

How Lime sees the World

#1

Lime was looking for our chickens and didn't see them. He said, "Chicken? No chicken." He looked some more and said "No horse". (We often can see horses in our neighbor's field.) He looked confused.

I asked him, "Where are they?"

Lime thought a moment and growled.

I asked "A tiger?"

Lime nodded and said, "Tiger," and growled. I'm assuming he meant that a tiger ate them because he said again, "No chicken, no horse," growled, and then said, "Tiger."

#2

Lime said, "I've got spiders in my hands. I got alligators in my pants."

I asked him, "Where are your tigers? Are your tigers in your tummy?"

To which he replied, "Yes! And they're scared!"

. . .

#3

Lime said as he extended his hand, "Look Mommy, a spider."

I responded unthinking, "Oh, let me see." He put a tiny, live spider in my hand. I gasped and brushed it off onto the floor. Lime looked confused at my reaction and started to look for the spider on the floor.

~

SLICE 4: A HANDFUL OF CHILDREN

Surprise Delivery

In labor with our fifth child.
My husband is an
experienced labor support.

We arrive at the hospital,
I'm four centimeters dilated but
handling contractions well.

The nurse assumes
I have a long time before
my baby comes.
She leaves with the promise
to check me in two hours.

I walk the room with Jesse.
We dance to silent music
and laugh at geeky jokes.
I brace myself when the

pain is sharp.

Then one contraction
hits like a cannonball
shot inside me.

My water breaks.
Jesse calls the nurse.
Moments later our baby is born.
Jesse catches him.

Doctor Daddy on call!

∽

A Hole in the Door

It's the hour before dinner—acid hour. I stir broccoli and hamburger at the stove, hoping to finish before any more of my five children fall apart.

"Mom," Cherry whines, "Lime won't get out the bathroom, and he's been in there forever!"

Lime, two years old and barely proficient at using the potty, does take his time. I turn the stove low and go to help him. The bathroom door opens enough to allow one finger through a gap and stops.

I hear a whimper. Whose bright idea was it to build a drawer that opens in front of a door?

"Lime, dear," I say, "are you all right?"

"The door won't open," he says.

"Close the drawer."

"I can't."

"Open the drawer and close it."

I hear the scratch as the drawer slides open and a slam. It stops short, still lodging the door shut.

Bother! Something is lodging the drawer open. "Lime," I say, trying to keep my voice calm, "can you empty the drawer?" Then I turn to Cherry. "Go turn off the stove." Dinner will have to wait.

I lie on the hall floor and look under the door. I see little feet run from the drawer to the bathtub. Hairbrushes and a hand mirror, a curling iron and toothpaste clatter into the porcelain tub. At least that's what I remember being in the drawer; I can't see any higher than his ankles.

"I'm making a big mess!" he comments cheerfully. I can imagine his bright smile. Usually I tell him to stay out of the drawer. Even empty, the drawer won't shut any further. Emptying the drawer should have worked! I jostle and jiggle the door, then thump it hard with my fist. Lime yelps. I drop my hand and lay my forehead against the wood.

Apple tugs on my arm. "Mommy, I'm hungry."

"Cherry!" My voice comes out shrill. "Go put a movie on for your siblings."

My baby starts to cry. He's only nine months old and a movie won't do much for him. I hastily put him in the high chair and give him some baby teething biscuits. He settles into smearing himself and the tray with partially masticated mush.

I grab a butter knife and run back to the bathroom door. Lime is whimpering again. I shove the butter knife through the slight opening of the door and drag it against the edge of the drawer, trying to draw it shut. And though I dull the tip of the knife, the drawer won't move.

It must be the towel rod we hung under the sink. It must have slid and jammed the drawer. "Can you move the towel holder?" I hope my panic doesn't come through.

A *clank, clank,* some crying and more clanking. "I can't," he cries. His cheerfulness has long since evaporated into hunger, like that of a caged animal. I look at my watch. He's been stuck for almost an hour.

I can't get to the door's hinge pins to pop them out. I can't open the door without closing the drawer. I can't close the drawer without moving the towel rod. I can't get to the towel rod, and my two-year-old can't move it. The bathroom has no window.

The only option left—cut the door.

I call my husband. "Um... Lime's stuck in the bathroom." I explain the situation. "Can you think of any other way than cutting the door?"

Silence and more silence, then, "Do you want me to come home to cut it?"

"No. I can get it cut before you get home. I'll just do it."

I gather the drill and jigsaw. I'm feeling calmer now that I can do something. "Lime, get in the bathtub and stay there."

I watch under the door. His stockinged feet scurry across the floor and disappear into the tub. Hairbrush, curling iron, hand mirror and toothpaste clank together. Hopefully the mirror is still in one piece and he won't cut himself. He's not crying. Even if he did cut himself, I couldn't do anything until I cut into the room.

I drill a large hole near the bottom of the door.

Lime starts crying.

The drill is loud, but the jigsaw will be louder. I push the jigsaw blade through the hole and start sawing. The door is hollow and cuts easily until I run into the framing at the edge. I ease the blade around a corner and start cutting a rough rectangle, about eighteen by nine inches.

Lime is wailing now.

I push the cut door piece through like a punch-out paper doll. It clings and protests then falls to the floor. Eighteen by nine inches is a tight squeeze, but I won't take time to cut more. I snake my way through and scoop my little one out of the bathtub. He blubbers in my arms for a moment and then looks at the hole, eyes wide. "Can I climb through?"

My other kids charge up the stairs. They each demand a turn to crawl through the cut door. And dinner is forgotten.

The garage door growls open, then footsteps echo up to the second floor. I feel my husband's arms wrap around me.

"You're amazing, you know that?" he whispers in my ear.

I turn around and bury my face in his shoulder, laughter and tears coming to the surface as I snuggle into his embrace.

He chuckles and kisses me. Then he bends down to look through the hole. "I didn't dare say it on the phone, but I kept hoping you'd say 'April Fools'."

I cut a hole in a door—the bathroom door—on April Fool's Day. It's no joke.

How the door got stuck.

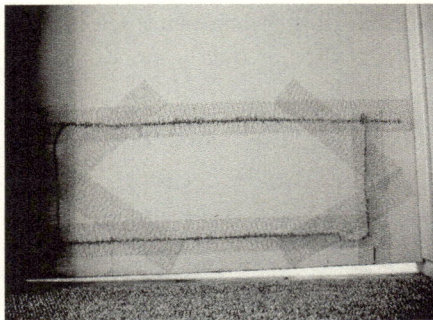

A little drywall tape (and later paint) and we had a whole door again.

BAKER'S TIPS: LESSONS LEARNED IN TEN YEARS OF MARRIAGE

Lessons on Marriage from Leo Tolstoy

The book *Anna Karenina* shows both the beauty of a faithful and loving marriage and the tragedy of infidelity (two different couples). The following thoughts are from part 5, chapter 14.

- Marriage is work and joy beyond anything you've experienced before.
- When you are married, you are one, and hurting your spouse also hurts yourself. Work through things together instead of fighting each other.
- Be patient and communicate. Don't let molehills grow to mountains.

∽

Not-So-Newlywed Game

Our church had a game night for the adults. We played the "Not-So-Newlywed" game. Jesse and I were one of four couples to compete. In this game, one spouse leaves the room while the other answers questions, then the spouse comes back and answers the same questions.

The object is to answer the question the same. Here are my two favorite questions and answers:

"What is your favorite memory of Maria—after marriage and birth of children?"

Jesse said, "Every day."

So when it came my turn to answer they said, "you'll never guess it, it is the sweetest answer ever, but you'll never guess it."

I thought then answered, "Every morning." It counted.

"What phrase does Jesse say all the time?"

I answered, "He says to me 'you're so cute!' all the time."

When Jesse answered, he said, "I say to Maria, 'You're so cute!'"

I didn't know his shoe size, and he didn't know my dress size, but in the important things, we knew each other.

∾

Peacemaker Patience

I would think that being a peacemaker and having patience go hand in hand. But they don't, not always, and for me—not often. I don't like contention or unresolved conflict. I try to talk it out immediately and find reconciliation. But I've learned repeatedly that when I push for that conversation before the other person has had time to think and process their emotions, it only exacerbates the situation.

This is especially true with Jesse. He takes time to think and feel through things, and he doesn't think in words. He's an artist and an engineer. He thinks in visual ideas. Before he can talk through things, he has to translate all those visuals into words. When I ask to talk about something right after it happens, he pulls away and finds a place away from me because he's processing and translating. But when he does speak, it is almost always thoughtful, relevant, and concise—if I give him the time. Only then can we discuss and find a resolution together.

So I've learned, and am still learning, to wait, to give space, to come back to it when we are both ready—which may be several days later. And even if those days are uncomfortable with silent processing and grim expressions, the resolution is worth the wait. And then we can come back to it and discuss it.

~

Observations of a good man

Thoughts pulled from my journal at around ten years into our marriage, when we had five children and the youngest was a baby.

Jesse uses gentle humor to help our children when they are grumpy. I can learn so much from him. Today when he helped Lime get ready for the day, Lime didn't want to. Jesse told him, "You have two choices, 'yes' or 'tickles.'"

Lime said, "No." So Jesse tickled him and Lime laughed and laughed.

Then Jesse said again, "You have two choices—'yes' or 'tickles'."

To which Lime said, "tickles?"

Jesse stays up talking with the kids at bedtime about whatever they want to.

When I made gingerbread cookies, I was exhausted by the end of the project. Jesse listened consolingly as I explained that I must not be a baker. I enjoy making meals, but baking takes more time and energy than I have right now. Then he said, "What if I'm the baker in the family? You be the chef and I'll take care of the desserts."

Last night Huckleberry was up all night, again. Jesse took him so I could get some sleep. Huckleberry cried and cried and fell asleep and then woke up and cried more. It was a hard night. So grateful for Jesse.

. . .

When a daughter asked us for examples of how learning pure doctrine changes our lives, Jesse talked about how at church he was listening and pondering what he needs to change in his life. Then he had the thought come: "What you need to work on is to not seek distractions". When Jesse said this, I had lots of thoughts go through my mind. Jesse used to go off into his own world with his Nintendo game system, but he hardly does that anymore. He is so much more involved and engaged in our family. His prayers are more fervent, he studies his Scriptures and listens to conference talks on the way to and from work. He is such a good man. He was a good man when I married him, and he keeps getting better. So his saying this helped me realize he is a humble man too. And because he is humble, he keeps improving. I hope I can be as humble and willing to change as he is.

Jesse worked hard through school so he could get employment that pays well, so I can stay home with our family. He also chose employment that he enjoys, so when the day is done he has the strength and energy to preside in our family. Jesse does so much for our family when he is home: he plays with the children; he listens to me; he helps with our many projects; he creates beauty. Jesse listens and holds me when I need to ramble and then offers comfort and suggestions when I ask for advice.

Our oldest daughter asked what we should do for Father's Day, and Jesse said, "I don't want anything big or that takes lots of preparation. I want to spend time with my family. So if we are going to do something big—like a cheesecake—I want to do it with you."

SLICE 5: CHILDREN TEACHERS

"While we try to teach our children all about life, our children teach us what life is all about."
—Angela Schwindt

Service

#1

In church we learned of a family with four boys who had moved into the area with nothing. I gathered kitchen tools, dishes, and linens, plus an extra chair. The kids ran around, going through their toys and stuffed animals. They were so excited to give to this family.

Pecan gave up several of his nice toys and kept going back for more to give. He said, "I want to give them these; they will like them."

Cherry gave them one of her stuffed animals that she loved. I told her she didn't need to, but she replied, "I love my husky, and I know they will too."

#2

On the morning of Valentine's Day, when the alarm went off, we heard some quiet noises in the kitchen. I went out to find Cherry and Apple making breakfast. Cherry had set her alarm to go off at 3 a.m. Then she fell back asleep, and they both got up at 5 a.m. They were all dressed in cute Valentine clothes, setting the table, making toast and excited to surprise us.

#3

Pecan got out his remote control car and stuck sticky notes with compliments to it, then drove them up to people. He called it his "compliment car".

~

Example

Pecan was teaching the family gospel lesson on example. He defined *a good example* as "Doing something good. And making it easy for others to follow." I like the second part of his definition. I usually just think of the first part, but the second part—making it easy for others to follow—is also important.

~

Christmas Joy

Christmas evening we focused our "thankfuls" on our Savior. I'm humbled by what my children said.

Cherry – He made it possible for families to be together forever.

Pecan – He was born. Because if He wasn't, He couldn't have died and been resurrected, and we would never be resurrected.

Apple – He created the earth. If He didn't, we'd never get bodies.

BAKER'S TIP: KINDNESS

A Prayer for Kindness

I was thinking about how I want to lift others up, but sometimes (especially when I'm tired) I fall into criticism instead.

Heavenly Father, please help me...
See my weaknesses so I:

- may be humble and draw closer to Thee
- may change and improve
- may have compassion for others in their struggles

See my strengths:

- that I may use them to lift others up and to build the kingdom of God

See the strengths of others:

- to recognize their strengths

- to praise at every opportunity

See the weaknesses and trials of others:

- to be compassionate and never critical
- to only speak correction sandwiched in love and praise
- to keep my mouth closed if the correction outweighs the love, until I can speak in pure love
- to never speak poorly of another behind their back
- give suggestions as suggestions—let them follow or not—and drop the topic myself

∼

Choice in Waiting

We eagerly looked forward to a community play, but we were running late getting out the door, and I had a choice of either being frustrated with the person who was keeping us from going, or to play with those in the van waiting. I chose to play the question game in the van and be at peace with the person in the bathroom. That choice made such a difference. We arrived ten minutes late, but we arrived in a happy mood.

SLICE 6: HALF A DOZEN CHILDREN

Strawberry is Here

Our sweet Strawberry arrived. A few days after she was born, seven of our chicks hatched. Apple said, "Both my wishes came true. I wanted a baby sister, and I wanted baby chicks."

~

Sillies

Lime asked to learn the "Toilet Trouble" song. Jesse translated for me; the lyrics are "Double, double, toil and trouble" from the *Harry Potter* movie (and, of course, Macbeth).

~

Cute Bug

Apple asked Lime what he was doing, and he said, "I'm playing with this bug."

Apple asked, "Is it alive?"

Lime replied matter-of-factly, "Yes."

Apple backed away. "Don't put it on me; keep it on yourself."

Lime tilted his head in confusion. "It's a cute bug...it's a super cute bug."

~

Bedtime Dragon

Lime told us he wanted his dragon drawing to stay above his bed, because it protected him. I asked if it protected him from bad dreams.

Lime shook his head. "No."

Cherry asked, "From the monsters under the bed?"

Lime said, "No—it protects me from bed bugs."

He has a very practical dragon.

~

Before I Knew Everything

Cherry responded to a question with, "It is probably before you knew everything." I laughed and explained I am far from knowing everything.

~

Spider Friend

Friend One

Lime told me that he didn't like to use the bathroom downstairs. I asked him why. He said, "I liked looking at the spider, but now the spider is gone."

I asked, "So you liked to use the restroom downstairs when it had a spider?"

Lime replied, "Yeah."

Sadly for Lime, the rest of us didn't like the spider in the bathroom, and I sent it the way of all the earth—in a flattened form.

Friend Two

Between sessions of General Conference, Lime caught and carried around a "smiley face spider" (bold jumping spider), letting it crawl over his hand and showing others. Then he put it in his treat cup so "it could have something to eat." No one would snitch from his treats.

~

Think About It

Part I

I've noticed that Cherry's response to many things—like, "Do you want to take art lessons?" is "I'll think about it". I'm grateful that she takes time to think about things before deciding. She is a very wise young lady.

Part II

At the splash park, Lime asked me, "Why didn't you bring me a change of clothes?"

I said, "Because..."

Lime finished for me, "Because I didn't ask you?"

Part III

Cherry said to Pecan, "Will you go find Apple and ask her where she is?" Cherry laughed as she realized what she'd said, then laughed harder when she heard Pecan say to Apple, "Where are you?" and Apple respond, "I'm right here!"

Part IV

When I told Lime that we were going to dye eggs, he asked, "Why are we going to kill the eggs?"

∾

Body of Silliness

Apple said, "The tongue is skin—that can taste. I'm glad my hands can't taste."

I said, "My ears are asleep," when I misheard someone.

Pecan replied, "If my ears were asleep, I'd hear them snoring."

Now, when we mishear, we often say, "My ears must have been snoring."

One day I pointed to Strawberry in the mirror and said, "Look, it's a cutie-pie".

Strawberry smiled, pointed at herself, and said, "Pie". For the next week, whenever she saw herself in the mirror, she pointed and said, "Pie".

∾

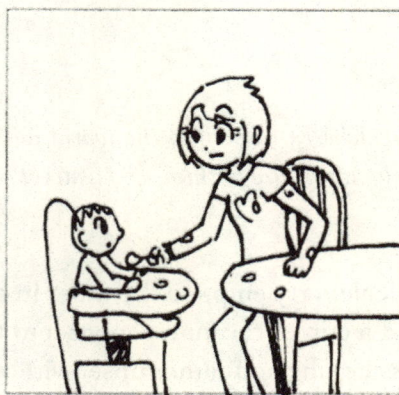

SLICE 7: ADVENTURES WITH HUCKLEBERRY

Huckleberry came into the world with an extra measure of energy. Life is a daily adventure for him, and a sweet one.

Huckleberry emptied the water in the teapot, a full pint of salt and kelp, and a cup of cayenne pepper into the frying pan. He was pleased with his cooking and rather upset with me when I poured it down the sink. I think he will be a good chef someday.

~

Huckleberry caught a fly and was holding it between two fingers. I told him to let it go, and the fly flew off, uninjured. There may be a reason I can't keep up with him. He's fast.

~

When Huckleberry catches a cold he seems determined to share it. He did lots of raspberries, so his spit went everywhere. Then he stuck his hand in two different water jugs, put his hands in the food as we prepared meals and then at the table when it was set, put dirty dishes in clean dishes... So it is unsurprising that we all caught colds shortly thereafter.

~

The most peaceful time of one day was reading out loud to the other kids while Huckleberry was in the bath. The peaceful time ended when I entered the bathroom to find half an inch of water covering the bathroom floor. Huckleberry had industriously bailed half the bathtub onto the floor with a large cup.

~

Huckleberry wanted the light on behind him, though he had one on overhead. He said, "I can't see."

I replied, "Yes, you can. You have a light."

To which he said, "But the back of my head can't see." He's developing the eyes in the back of his head early.

~

I told Huckleberry, "Go tell Pecan that Mommy would like him to come."

He went to Pecan and said, "Pecan, Mommy likes you."

~

Huckleberry said, "Mommy, you're so pretty," then added, "do you have wings?"

~

The boys' room had a funny smell one evening. We looked around until we found a dead mouse in the back of the boys' closet. Huckleberry, age four, explained that he'd killed the mouse with the laundry basket a few days before. We found mouse fur on the basket so I trust that is really what happened.

BAKER'S TIPS: PARENTING LESSONS WITH SIX KIDS

Families are forever. Tantrums are not.

∾

Multitasking

Multitask things but never people. Give people my full attention. Stop what I'm doing and do not let thoughts interrupt or distract. Working hard on this one.

∾

Prime Real Estate

The tabletop is prime real estate in our family of eight. It is often only clear of projects in the moments before setting it for a meal.

∾

Be Understandable

> I had rather speak five words with my understanding, that by my voice
> I might teach others also, than ten thousand words in an unknown
> tongue.
> —1 Cor. 14:19

Speak in words that others can understand and in simplicity. Our Savior said, "Love one another." Three simple words that change lives. Lincoln's Gettysburg Address is half a page of a clear and powerful call to action.

SLICE 8: FAMILY ADVENTURES

We've never been to Disneyland or camped at Yellowstone. But we've had adventures much grander—time with family in Idaho, Utah, Oregon, Washington, Connecticut and Canada. Playing games with cousins. Laughing around the dinner table with aunts and uncles. Snuggling up to grandparents. Adventures with family.

Here are some of many:

~

New Year on the Beach

We bundle into my parents' van—Jesse, our toddler, all my siblings, a brother's girlfriend, and I—ten of us in total. The beach is two hours from my childhood home. Poetry flits. We toss verses like a frisbee. "Jabberwocky", "The Cremation of Sam McGee", "The Turkey Shot out of the Oven", the Gettysburg Address. We laugh and ponder in turns. The drive ends too soon.

We watch for whales and see a seal. The waves crash gray under a gray sky. A brother flips a rock into the trough between waves, and it skips. We all compete, or attempt to. Most stones sink into the foam.

The tide goes out, leaving behind mussel-encrusted stones. Dad and the boys clamber down with buckets and pocket knives. One stands watch, calling a warning when a big wave rolls in. They all grab the stones as the water splashes over them, then, as it drains in rivulets, they continue their shellfish collecting.

When we return, we find a shallow stream running from the cliff, through the high beach, to the ocean. It cuts across our way to the van. Dad hoists me on his back and carries me across. I'm more wet from the piggyback ride than I'd have been wading, but I giggle like a little girl riding her daddy's shoulders.

Cherry follows in her daddy's arms and giggles just as much.

~

Family Reunion on the Coast

Splash One
Swimming pool rings with laughter,
blind Marco catching splashing Polos.
Everyone playing, except my three-year-old son.

He sits on the edge, yelling directions:
"No running, don't splash, be careful,"
until our laughter draws him in.

He steps into the shallow end,
giggling as water laps against his legs,
then plunges after his sister,
his life vest bobbing him on
splash-created ripples.
"Polo!"

Splash Two
Oregon Coast means rain,
even in August.
We build a driftwood campfire

as dark clouds build overhead.

Flames pop and snap
around misting rain.
We add the sizzling drips of
roasting hot dogs.

We keep damply warm,
filling the air with camp songs
and flaming marshmallows.

Splash Three
We hunt for agates
along the base of the sea cliffs.
Our baby, a permanent fixture on my hip,
demands down.

She sits upon a pile of
colored, translucent stones,
a dragon on her horde,
and growls happily.

Splash Four
Impromptu talent show,
started unintentionally by Great-grandpa,
when he tells us, "I got my shoes at JCPenney."

We act out the scout skit "JCPenney".
When he stands to do his part,
he whispers, "What are we doing?"
Grandmama whispers back, "Improvising."

Laughter overwhelms words.

∾

Canada

A two-day drive to see
Great-grandma Yaeko,
crossing country borders
to celebrate her 88th birthday.

Grandma Yaeko teaches
Pecan to juggle.
At seven, he's as tall as she is
and she is quicker than any of us.

∼

Solar Eclipse

Tents mound like colored mushrooms over sagebrush desert. Sawtooth mountains cut the sky around us. Families gather from many states to watch the solar eclipse, and more importantly, to be together. I see my cousins, who now have their own kids. The next generation of children chase each other over the dusty ground.

We hike Abe's Chair. The last time I'd made the hike was before I had children. This time I do it carrying my sixth and youngest child. My little sister does the same with her baby. Five miles up the side of a mountain with no trail—steep slopes, fallen trees to climb over, wildflowers, shale, and at the top a ten-foot-wide peak with cliffs on three sides.

Songs around the campfire echo words that were sung years ago. The family clan, spread through four generations, is more than kin—we are friends bound together by memories, laughter, and love.

∼

Family Reunion in the Mountains

It doesn't take much to be happy:

three-legged races,
water fights with sponges,
hide-and-seek in the bushes.

Little girls build
a fairy house with bark and leaves,
setting out blossom beds.

Three boys look like puppies
with dirt-patched skin.
Only their grins are white and eyes bright.

Hikes; spotting moose, hawks, and deer;
balancing on fallen tree trunks,
seeing how far we can go without touching the ground.

Skits and jokes.
Family stories around the fire.
Passing on tales of before.

SLICE 9: HOME ADVENTURES

Broken AC

July is hot,
high 90s in the day,
low 80s at night.
We like our AC.

Then it breaks.

We change our meals to salads,
and hang clothes on a line to dry.
The deck is a riot of color on laundry day.

We discover how to best place fans,
circulating air through the house,
and visit many splash parks.

Summer necessity is the mother of invention.

~

Early Halloween Visitor

3 a.m.
A fluttering sound.
A bat flies frantic figure eights
in our living room.

We drive it toward an open door.
It swerves around to
return to the biggest room,
squeaking its fright.

Jesse catches it with a laundry basket.
It escapes, crawling through the holes.
Finally we stun it with a whiteboard.

Poor bat.
We like them because they eat mosquitoes.
We just don't want one in our house.

We had guests staying downstairs, and in the morning they asked about all the noise. I promised we don't usually run around throwing laundry baskets and whacking things with dry erase boards in the middle of the night.

P.S. For those who wonder, animal control picked it up and tested it—it had no diseases.

~

3 a.m. Burglar

A burglar tried to break into our garage. He wore a black mask, and I think he was after the cat food. But he was too big to fit through the cat door, so he tried to tear apart the door itself, and he half-succeeded. Raccoons!

Our house is about 50 years old. We'd been meaning to replace that garage door at some point—it was a hollow-core door. But we live out in a farming area and felt safe, so we kept putting it off. We spent the next two days ripping out the old door and frame (which had rotted) and installing a new frame and door in a brick doorway that wasn't square. We had to take it out and redo it because it was so off-kilter the first time that the door wouldn't latch.

3 a.m. must be our animal intruder hour.

~

Nighttime Rooster

A wild rooster decided to settle in the pine outside our bedroom window, and he thought it best to wake the world at 2 a.m. After three nights of throwing sticks and rocks at him until he flew away, and having him come back the next night, I said, "If he doesn't stop crowing, he's going to be soup." He must have heard our plans, because we never heard him again after that night.

~

Guardian Angels

After dinner we sat down to a game of Apples to Apples.

Huckleberry watched for a bit and then said to his little sister, "Come on, Strawberry, let's go on an adventure."

They played peek-a-boo and blanket ghosts, then things grew quiet.

We found them in the garage in the midst of their biggest adventure —and one that made me grateful for guardian angels. Huckleberry had climbed onto the freezer, pulled two jars of cherries from the shelf, and broken one of them on the cement floor. It was only the bottom that was broken, and the glass looked to be in several large pieces. What scared me was the cherry pits all over the floor. They'd eaten a good amount of the cherries.

But he and Strawberry didn't have one cut on them—hands, feet, or mouth. I'm so grateful! I'm grateful for Heavenly Father's protection!

~

Plumbing

Plumbing repair is my nemesis. I'm grateful I don't have to battle it very often. One of these days I'll actually call Jesse at work and ask him to come home to address the leak. In the end it works out, but I feel as though I've fought an arch-villain who pulled every dirty trick in the book, including water torture in claustrophobic conditions.

~

Stream in our Living Room

When Strawberry started eating the plaster flaking from the 17-foot-long fireplace bench, we decided it was time to replace it with a wooden storage bench.

Day 1
Couches and a sideways piano bench
barricade half the room.
Toddler stands watching
while we
chip away plaster,
tear out drywall,
and fill the air with white.

We are ghostly workers,
wielding hammers and chisels.

Day 2
A slivery frame of two-by-fours
opens to an insulated wall.
With exact care,
Pecan pries up the old plywood bench,
preserving it to use again.

Day 3
Sand, cut, paint.

Cover the insulated wall.
Brace the two-by-fours.
The framework is
no longer a sliver and fiberglass hazard.

Day 4
Cutting four-by-eight sheets of plywood
is a balancing act.
Cherry spreads the panels on plastic
and paints grass, sprinkling it with flowers.
A cat hides in the meadow.

Day 5
Little boys paint base coats of blue.
One paints a blue bear,
then hides it in the blue stream.

We attach the meadow panels
to the front of the bench.
Our living room is still a construction zone,
but now we have a meadow to cheer up the space.

Day 6
Koi swim and leap in a stream,
each freehand painted
on the removable bench seats.

The kids hide in the bench
and pop out like
gophers in the meadow
or otters in the stream.

Everyone helped with the project, from tearing out, to new construction, to painting, and even watching the toddler so she didn't get into the middle of it.

~

Life Cycle of a Rough Draft

I've written hundreds of thousands of words in rough drafts. The papers join the home adventures in a life cycle of their own.

When I've typed the last word of the final chapter, revised, edited, and can't bear to stare at the screen another moment, I print out the manuscript. Weeks later, with a marked-up, scribbled-on stack of papers, I type my changes back into the computer.

Then I drop the obsolete draft onto the scratch paper pile. Two-hundred-plus pages, storied on front and blank on the back, each ready for the next stage in its life.

To what destiny?

Some draft pages are chosen by Cherry. She started drawing people at age two and hasn't stopped since. Every scrap of paper, edges of spelling lists, and end pages of books she owns are covered in people, creatures, and scenes. As soon as she's done eating, she grabs a paper from the scratch pile, a pen or a brush, and draws while carrying on dinner conversation with the rest of us. As we watch lines take life, the conversation pauses. She shrugs at our comments, finishes the drawing and tucks it back into the scratch paper pile. She's created for the joy, not the keeping.

Sometimes I rescue the drawing to tuck into a portfolio. But often the papers continue on to their next stage. Apple pulls out a sketch, holds it to the window with a blank paper over top and traces, adding her own sweet style. Strawberry grabs another sketch and crayons it in, happily reporting on "cats", "oh pretty" and "dragons." All horses are dragons to her.

Other draft pages are the canvas for math problems, teased out between mind and pen. Numbers crowd against numbers. Scribbles of frustration or big inked stars showing *I've finally got it*. Pecan swaps between imaginary and educational journeys of the mind. Castles and maps invade the paper's borders. The two journeys blur together, as numbers morph into castle stones, mirroring a similar struggle and journey on the opposite side of the page.

On some, Lime copies out plants and animals from the *Smithsonian Natural History*. While Huckleberry covers the paper, blank side and story side, in thick interconnecting lines of markers—his mazes to stump me.

Torn strips of draft paper become bookmarks. My novel's hero tucked into *Hop on Pop*, *Dinotopia*, *Ella Enchanted*, and *How Things Work*.

Shopping lists, jotted out directions, origami. Pinata paper-mache. Table shields under painted pumpkins.

Art and more art. Fairies flit on the back of battle scenes. Marker dragons leak through, and shadow treks through the desert. In some future, will someone turn over a saved piece of art to see the hero's love, the villain closing in, and ask—what happened next?

Even new stories take birth on the backs of old ones. My middle daughter chews on her pencil, then scribbles in scenes from her imaginary world of Sara and Ben. My oldest son plots world maps, naming each land for its resources. My firstborn designs races—part animal, part human—notating the size, diet, abilities, and personalities along the margins. Phoenix rising from paper ashes.

Once, when paper and canvas were expensive, the artist painted over old art. In our family, we follow a similar path. Not because of cost, but because of the thought, *I can create whatever I want on this page, and if I mess up it doesn't matter, it's just scratch paper.* And creations abound.

My stories become canvas for their art,
And their lives are the canvas for my stories.

INTO THE OVEN: TRIPLE BAKE

Twice-baked potatoes are baked once, then the center is scooped out and mixed with other yummy ingredients, put back into the skin, and baked again. It is a delicious, rich, crispy, creamy treat. It requires both bakes.

This following period of my life felt like a triple bake. I've changed into a better person because of it. I'm grateful I didn't know that one would come right after the other. A mercy of not knowing the future.

~

Bake 1: Surgery and Trusting God's Answers

I'd been getting more and more tired since before Strawberry was born. It came on slowly, and so I didn't realize how much it had progressed until Strawberry was almost two. I attributed it to pregnancy, then new baby, then kids not sleeping through the night, and then taking care of six kids, etc. I finally went into the doctor about it because I was also getting lightheaded.

The doctor discovered that I had some major women's health issues, which were making me anemic and were progressively getting worse. We were given several options for what we could do as temporary measures, but the end result sooner or later would be a major surgery—one that would mean we wouldn't have any more children.

Jesse and I filled the following weeks with prayer, fasting, temple attendance, pondering, and studying. We received a sweet assurance that I should have the surgery and not to wait. That sweet peace carried me through nights of insomnia, worried days, doubts and fears, and a range of the frailties of human emotion.

I learned that Heavenly Father helps me in my frailties even as Satan does his utmost to make me doubt spiritual impressions.

My journal is full of entries like:

- *I know I received peace and assurance that we should do what the doctor recommended. I'm trying to hold to that faith and not let doubt and second-guessing overwhelm me.*
- *I'm feeling much better today. I thank Heavenly Father for the experience of anxiety yesterday and then peace. I know He loves me. I know He's answered my questions regarding what we should do. I know He also lets me experience human emotions of anxiety to help grow my faith. I hope not to experience that anxiety again, but if I do, I'll hold true to what I know and I'll turn to Him for help.*
- *I've been feeling really good the last couple days, better than I have in months—and so I start having second thoughts again for a different reason. Thoughts that maybe I don't need the surgery, maybe it is unwise to have something so major done. And then I remember the answer I received in the temple and I know that was a clear and sweet calming answer. And I know that I should doubt not, marvel not what the Lord can do—even giving me greater health before the surgery.*

And through all these emotions I've felt Heavenly Father's sweet peace, when I could "be still" enough to feel it. I am so grateful for Heavenly Father's tender care over me through this time. I've grown so close to Him and my testimony of His personal love and individual care for me has grown stronger. The journal entries above don't show a very strong person, but He carried me in my weakness.

It was really good that we didn't wait on the surgery. I lost several times as much blood as is usual for this type of surgery, and if we'd waited, it probably would have been even worse. After the surgery, my emotions quieted and I felt peace.

When I was a single college student, my dad gave me advice on hearing and acting on God's directions. He counseled that when I pray about something and receive an answer, to write it down, so when I face doubts I can read the answer and remember. This advice has helped me many times through my life, and perhaps most in the time before the surgery.

∾

Bake 2: Tachycardia

Less than a year later, I went in for a regular doctor checkup and found that I was experiencing a very high heart rate. After three EKGs, a stress test, thyroid test, nutritional questionnaire, heart ultrasound, and many days of wearing a chest heart monitor, the cardiologist diagnosed my condition as *inappropriate tachycardia*, meaning they could find no reason physically, nutritionally, hormonally, or otherwise that I should have the tachycardia, but I had it.

Inappropriate Tachycardia

I laugh at the name
"Inappropriate" tachycardia.
When is it ever appropriate?

My heart thinks it's a race car.

Engine revs on waking.
I go from 60 BPM to 120.
All it takes is to rise from bed and
walk down the hall.

My heart jumps out the starting gate
like a racehorse.
Jogging takes it from
110 to 176 BPM in
half a minute.

I rest in the 60s,
I walk in the 110s,
I exercise in the 170s.
This is life with a racing heart.

And yet I have every
reason to be grateful.
My heart is strong,
my family supportive, and
God is filling my life with grace.

The cardiologist helped me make a plan for living with this new challenge, which included permission to do regular life as long as I paid attention and slowed down when needed. As a mother of six, I needed both the permission and the warning. Thankfully those measures alleviated the worst of the tachycardia, and life mostly went back to normal.

A few months *before* I learned about my tachycardia, I wrote out my New Year resolutions. I felt that I'd fully healed from the surgery and I was ready to dive back into life at full speed. As I prayed to know where to focus, I felt a specific instruction: *Do not add more on my plate of to-dos, but rather focus on the more important parts. Draw closer to God. Be more focused in my time with my children and husband. Serve.*

Heavenly Father was preparing me for further life changes.

∽

Bake 3: Syncopated Heart

A year after my initial heart tests a nasty flu rampaged through our home. Afterwards, my wrist heart monitor started showing drops down to 30 BPM as well as jumps to the 170s. During the slow heart rate periods a sluggish thump vibrated through my entire body, including my teeth. I also experienced my very first migraines. My regular doctor said that slow of heart rate was dangerous and I might need a pacemaker. I was only 37 years old. Despite my tachycardia, I was healthy, athletic, and full of dreams for life. This wasn't what I wanted to hear.

It led to soul pondering. As I waited for results from further testing, I wrote in my journal:

What would I need to do to prepare my family and put my life in order if I were to be called home to heaven?

- *Spiritual: Record my testimony, bear my testimony. Encourage my family to follow Christ, keep on the covenant path, and learn to hear and act on personal revelation. Serve.*
- *Relationship: Time with my husband and each child individually and all together. Love, laughter, listen, be with. See all my immediate family again.*

Bucket list (if I have the time on earth, then I will do these things):

- *Raise all my children to adulthood.*
- *Serve church missions with Jesse.*

Bucket list (these are things I'd love to do but are not necessary):

- *Finish any partially written books. Keep writing.*
- *Visit Japan with Jesse.*

The above list has helped me decide where to focus in my day-to-day. I'm grateful for the time of uncertainty to truly evaluate what is important.

The cardiologist found that I had developed ventricular ectopy, or syncopated beats, which were giving my wrist heart monitor a false low. Though exhausting, the syncopated beats were not life threatening, nor did they require surgery. Further adjustments in my activities and medication helped alleviate much of this new development.

Now I go through life with a jazzy heart that likes to race. Some days are difficult. Yet I feel truly blessed by Heavenly Father's many mercies and His guidance in my life.

~

Refiner's Fire

He shall sit as a refiner and purifier of silver: and he shall purify the sons of Levi, and purge them as gold and silver, that they may offer unto the Lord an offering in righteousness.
—Malachi 3:3

Refining is not done so much out of judgment but out of mercy. God knows our potential and gives us the necessary trials and learning experiences to refine and purify us. It is for our sake—whether to bring us to repentance; to refocus us; or to teach us spiritual gifts like compassion, charity, closeness to God, and complete trust in Him.

He's very loving and careful in what trials He sends us. It's not as though He just throws us into the furnace of affliction and then goes to lunch. He's beside us every step of the way, comforting, strengthening, and helping.

SLICE 10: CHILDREN'S WIT AND WISDOM

One morning I woke Pecan by saying, "Wake up! The sun is on fire!"

He groaned, "Of course it is."

I used the same line on Cherry, and she said, "It's a good thing, or we'd be really cold."

~

Huckleberry ran into the kitchen and said, "Pecan needs amentawrench."

I was completely confused. "A what?"

"A-ment-a-wrench."

Pecan came in and explained. "I said, I need some tweezers, no I meant a wrench." Then he grabbed pliers.

I guess he needed "a-ment-a-pliers."

~

We were talking about someone famous, and Lime said, "Well, he may be all that, but," and by his tone of voice I expected him to say: *but I'm superman.* Instead, he said, "Well, he may be all that, but I'm a rubber ducky."

~

Apple said, "I just can't figure out these dementors!" She was talking about denominators in fractions. But to some people denominators are pretty demented.

~

Huckleberry asked, "Do you know how fast I ran? I made a sonic boom!"

~

Lime told me this riddle: "When does 2 + 2 = 22? When you have 2 dimes and 2 pennies."

~

Jesse asked Cherry to say the family prayer one morning. She folded her arms, closed her eyes, and said, "Good Night". It took long minutes before we stopped laughing enough to pray together.

~

Jesse, Cherry, Pecan, and I played Phase 10 one evening while the younger kids watched a movie. When it was bedtime, I commented, "Who is brave enough to attempt to turn off the movie?"

Pecan said, "I will," and he ran down the stairs quietly screaming, as though he was running into a jungle. He got halfway then called up, "I couldn't do it!" We all busted up laughing.

~

Pecan was chopping onions, and they irritated his eyes. He ran out of the room yelling, "My eyes don't know what is good for them!"

∾

I called one of the kids by the wrong name (as I often do). I said, "I really do know your names."

Cherry rejoined, "But your tongue doesn't. It doesn't see us much."

∾

Huckleberry asked me just before he entered the bathroom, "Can you turn down the volume of the toilet?"

∾

Ever since Cherry could walk, she's loved to walk around in random patterns while she pretended. She coined it "thinky-thinking." I know she's really excited about something she's imagining when I hear a bang as she accidentally crashes into the wall. Lime picked up on the habit, though he does it outside.

INTO THE OVEN: DYSLEXIA

Lime has dyslexia, and we'd been working on learning to read for several years. Then my Grandma Stewart mentioned how my sister learned to read from the Holy Scriptures. So we added that to his reading lessons. The following miracle happened.

Two years trying to learn to read,
he still stumbles over "and" and "the".
"p", "b", and "d" are mirrors of the
same shape but different sounds.

Slowly, bit by bit, sounding out
moving letters. He asks,
"Just half a lesson today?"

We make it to lesson 60 out of the 100 lessons.
Halted at the same place as last year,
when we took a summer break before trying again.
How to learn past this mountain?

He's not my first child, nor this the first

"tried and true" method to teach reading.

He's smart.
He's motivated.

But the letters swim,
slipping away from him as he
grasps their slick sides.

Then sweet words from my Grandma Stewart:
"Remember how your sister learned to read?"

I open the book, the one he's heard
every day since he was in the womb.

I run my fingers under the words
"I, Nephi, having been born of goodly parents."
I read each word and have him repeat,
then ask him to sound out "having".
One word read in a line, a big word.
He grins.

Many minutes later he recognizes "of."
It doesn't swim away.
"And" still causes trouble.
But he reads three verses with me.

The next day and the next
we open the Scriptures and read.
"And it came to pass as he prayed unto the Lord."
He sounds out a whole line with
only help on "prayed"

"Mommy, I'm reading!
I like this so much better than the

reading lesson book.
But the words are longer and harder.
Why is this easier?"

"Why?" I catch at the tears.
"Because this book is
Heavenly Father's book.
He wants us to read it.
He is helping you."

My son tells his five-year-old brother
"You should learn to read from the
Book of Mormon.
The Holy Ghost will help you."

His first testimony,
born out of the trials of dyslexia.

Since then he's slowly and surely progressed in his reading through
the help of teachers and family. I'm so grateful for God's tender
mercies!

SLICE 11: STRAWBERRY SPOTLIGHT

Strawberry didn't learn to walk until she was almost eighteen months old. Though she could stand steady and occasionally took a few steps, she was content with crawling or being carried. That is, until one day she watched her brothers run through the house, sword fighting. She crawled after them, dragging a toy sword; and finally, with a determined look, stood up and toddled after them, waving her sword. Cherry said, "A little girl picks up her sword and takes her first step."

～

Strawberry could identify a dragon before she could identify a horse. She'd been calling a stuffed animal zebra a dragon for about a week. When she saw a picture of a horse, she called it dragon, and then Cherry said, "Horse". Strawberry looked confused and then looked at the zebra and said, "Horse".

～

One evening when I said, "Bedtime," she cried out, "Oh no! Not again!"

~

Strawberry decided to decorate the carpet, one couch, and parlor table with a permanent marker. We spent the next hour undecorating said items while listening to the soundtrack of *Mission Impossible*.

~

Strawberry filled up play dishes with water and went into the parlor. I ran after her and asked, "Strawberry, are you getting into trouble?"

She responded, "Stop, Mom! I want to get into trouble."

~

Strawberry held out her hands to Daddy, as if she were holding something by its corners, and said "Here, a smile." Daddy leaned forward and she placed it on his face.

~

Strawberry crawled under the bunkbed and said, "I'm a monster." I guess she'll never be scared of monsters under the bed.

~

I was feeding Strawberry so she would finish her dinner. She covered her ears while she ate. Jesse asked, "Strawberry, are you covering your ears so you don't smell your food?" She nodded.

~

Strawberry came up to me and held out her hand. Her fingers were curved with the thumb pointing downward. She said, "Mommy, my heart is broken. You need to fix my heart."

As I stood confused, Apple laughed and came over. "Mommy, this is how you do it." Apple held up her hand, curved it like Strawberry's, and set it next to Strawberry's, forming a full heart.

Strawberry exclaimed, "You did it! You fixed my heart!"

∾

Strawberry washed her hands and said, "The spiders took a bath," then crawled her fingers across the counter to the hand towel.

∾

After I made a spicy salad dressing for a taco salad, Strawberry grabbed the lid and started licking it. After she'd had several licks, I put it by the sink. She cried out, "Let me lick the sugar!" The funny thing is it was lime juice, olive oil, garlic, onion, cayenne, cumin, salt, and chili powder—nothing sweet at all.

∾

Mix and Match Nativities

Seven nativity sets:
felt, stone, ceramic,
one thimble-sized,
Precious Moments,
squeezable dolls,
nesting Matryoshka.
Some fragile, some not.

We set the felt and doll sets low,
for our children to play with.
The other four find high shelves.

Three-year-old watches wide-eyed,
then drags a stool to each shelf

and carefully takes the sets down.

She gathers the many Marys
around baby Jesus.
They talk about their baby
and their day.
The Josephs stand guard.

The wise men all lie down
to sleep under the Christmas tree.

The shepherds chase their
flocks across the room.

Then she gently takes my hand,
and tells me the story of Christmas.

SLICE 12: GROWING UP

Children come into the world with personality and then grow quickly into their talents and interests. They surprise me, delight me, and cause me to scratch my head in bemusement. I cry over them, pray for them, and hope that they will find joy in whatever they choose to pursue. Most of all, I hope that they will follow Christ and love their neighbor.

~

Joyful Prize

Lime's school was doing a raffle for a virtual reality headset, and kids got tickets by doing well in school. Lime worked hard to get as many tickets as he could. He told me, "If I get it, I want to give it to Daddy for Christmas. He'll really like it!"

A few weeks later, Lime ran out of the school building with a huge grin on his face and said, "I'm the luckiest person in the school! I won the big prize!"

He almost exploded with excitement watching Daddy open it on Christmas Day.

Lime has dyslexia and school is difficult for him, which made this even more sweet.

Budding Author

Apple decided to become an author. She's written many fairy tales with her own twist: *Little White Writing Hood, The Girlabuman, The Three Big Monsters and the Scary Little Thing,* and more. I'm excited to see where she goes from here.

Snowman armor

Pecan and Lime stayed outside all afternoon playing in the snow. Then Pecan called me to take pictures. When I got out, I only saw Pecan and asked, "Where's Lime?" Pecan grinned and took the head off the snowman. Lime popped out. The two of them had rolled the balls, built the snowman, then hollowed it out. They made an air hole, which they covered with the snowman's scarf. Instead of a snow fort, they'd built snow armor.

~

How Cherry Sees the World

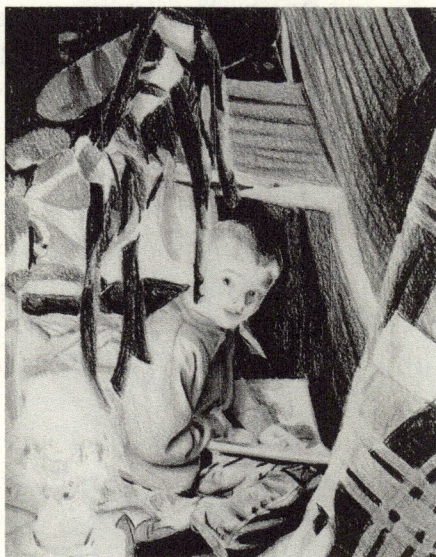

~

Mud Puddle Jumpers

Marjorie Pay Hinckley said, "The only way to get through life is to laugh your way through it. You either have to laugh or cry. I prefer to laugh. Crying gives me a headache."[1]

I dropped the kids off at school a few minutes before the doors opened to let in the first students. Once home, Strawberry and I started into her preschool, and then the phone rang.

"Hello. This is SAA. Is this Mrs. Farb?"

"Yes."

"We have Lime and Huckleberry Farb sitting in our office...."

...Oh no, what happened, did they...

"...they were wrestling in the mud. Could you bring down a change of clothes for both of them?"

First surprised words out of my mouth: "Where did they find mud?" We hadn't had rain for more than a month and it had been 95 - 100-degree weather.

She chuckled, "I don't know. I wonder that myself. But they both need a change of pants and shirt."

I grabbed the clothes from their closet and headed out the door. When I arrived, they were sitting in the office like a Norman Rockwell painting. They lifted their faces and looked at me with big brown puppy eyes. Mud smeared their foreheads and cheeks, accentuating their hesitant and apologetic looks. Mud daubed their pandemic-required face masks, green polo shirts and navy blue pants. Huckleberry had an extra coating slathered down his arms and his red shoes. Their backpacks had taken on earth tones.

I knelt in front of them and quietly asked. "Lime. Huckleberry. What happened?"

Huckleberry answered first. "We slipped in the mud."

"And how did that happen?"

Huckleberry dropped his gaze and Lime answered. "We were wrestling."

I held in my laughter, glad for the required mask to hide my mouth. Of all the things to be called into the school office for, this was a good one. They were being boys but not in trouble. "Come on. Let's go get changed and get you to class. Remember, no wrestling, and go straight to class next time. I'll make sure to not drop you off at school until the doors are open."

After they got all cleaned up, I sent them to class and returned to the office with an armful of muddy clothes. The secretary chuckled as I apologized again. "I have four boys," she said, "and I get this. No worries."

All the way home I laughed.

BAKER'S TIPS: LESSONS IN MANY YEARS OF MARRIAGE

Opposites

Opposites attract, but what keeps them together?

He majored in Electrical Engineering.
I majored in English.
We studied physics and calculus together.

He enjoys video games
and I reading.
We both love a good story.

He grew up working late into the night.
I usually can't sleep past 4:30 a.m.
We support each other when tired.

I work at high speeds.
He is precise in all he does.
Together we have any project covered.

I pull thoughts from all over.
He condenses ideas to their essential points.
We come to understand in breadth and depth.

I read out loud to our children.
He plays with them.
We build memories.

Together we
Pray
Counsel
Nurture
Work
Serve

Together we Love.

~

Happily Ever After

I read a short autobiography by Winston Churchill of his younger days. I loved how he ended it. Even writing it from the perspective of enduring two major world wars, he wrote, "Then I married and lived happily ever after."[1] No matter the darkness of the world, he kept this perspective.

Even though we haven't been happy every moment of our marriage, I can truly say Jesse and I are living happily ever after. We still have many faults and things we have to be patient about (with ourselves, each other, and just life). But we also have reached a level of trust where we can tell each other anything. We work through our struggles and growing experiences together. Our eternal goals are the same.

I think that having this trust and these same goals has helped us grow closer together instead of further apart when challenges arise. Our marriage isn't perfect, but it is wonderful, and it continues to grow more wonderful! Jesse is my best friend, my confidant, my fellow disciple of Christ.

I want to walk the eternities with him.

BAKER'S TIPS: SOME FINAL PARENTING THOUGHTS

Perspective

In our kitchen, we pinned two quotes next to each other.

Successful marriages and families are established and maintained on principles of faith, prayer, repentance, forgiveness, respect, love, compassion, work, and wholesome recreational activities.
—The Family: A Proclamation to the World

Success consists of going from failure to failure without loss of enthusiasm.
—Winston Churchill

We put them side by side so we can remember, as we strive for a successful family, that we will have many failures and mistakes along the way, and that we must keep going and growing without losing hope or enthusiasm.

~

Parenting Goals Worksheet

If I had only one sheet of paper outside of the Scriptures for parenting advice, I'd choose "The Family: A Proclamation to the World"[1].

This is a parenting goal worksheet I created from it:

Parenting Goals
Example of (how we act)
- love: _____
- righteousness: _____
Provide for children's needs
- physical: _____
- spiritual: _____
Teach children to
- love one another: _____
- serve one another: _____
- keep commandments of God: _____
- keep laws of land: _____

Principles of a Happy Family
Faith in Christ: _____
Prayer: _____
Repentance:_____
Forgiveness: _____
Respect: _____
Love: _____
Compassion: _____
Work: _____
Wholesome Recreation: _____

We wrote in specific actions on each blank. For example, by forgiveness, we have *hugs, gentle words, patience, and increased love.*

Because every family is different, every family will have different things to put in the blanks.

~

Children's Choices

Parenting is like being a missionary. I cannot take credit for good children. Their conversion is because of their choices and the converting power of the Holy Ghost. But I want to do all I can to raise them in an environment where they will hear God's guidance and know the choices and their consequences.

BAKING A LIFE PIE

ESSENTIAL AND BONUS INGREDIENTS

Every pie has a list of ingredients. This section is filled with ingredients that are essential parts of our family life, and some ways that we apply them. This is a snapshot of our specific family, and maybe some things will apply in your life. But not all of them will. You probably apply these and other ingredients in wonderful ways that are vastly different than ours, and that are perfect for your family.

Remember, the same ingredients combined in different proportions, perhaps with the addition of others, result in different but equally delicious desserts.

INGREDIENT: FAITH IN CHRIST

And we talk of Christ, we rejoice in Christ, we preach of Christ, we prophesy of Christ, and we write according to our prophecies, that our children may know to what source they may look for a remission of their sins.

—2 Ne 25:26

When we married we received dishes, linens, a basket of cleaning supplies, games, and even a *Princess Bride* DVD. But the one gift that we've carried from apartment to apartment and kept central in each of our homes is a figurine of the resurrected Christ. We've carefully packed it with each move. We've glued a hand back on from the time a curious child dropped it.

It stands in the midst of our family pictures, a reminder of our Savior, His great love for us, and His central place in our family.

Our family is founded on Christ. Some days, keeping firmly founded on Him feels like a battle. The world is always louder, more insistent, and in our faces. It is easy to let the work, school, projects, social events, or any number of other good and important things take center focus.

In order to keep our focus in Christ, we seek to know Him, trust Him, put Him first, and obey Him.

> "Jesus died and was resurrected
> so we can die and be resurrected and
> live with Heavenly Father again."
> —Cherry (age 7)

~

Seek to Know Christ

And this is life eternal, that they might know thee the only true God, and Jesus Christ, whom thou hast sent.
—John 17:3

How can we believe and trust someone we don't know? What if a stranger came up to me and started telling me what to do? At best, I'd be incredulous. At worst, I'd call the police. Yet if someone I knew and trusted did the same, I'd consider what they were saying. It is the same with Christ. He gives me commandments and direction—but if I don't know Him, then why would I trust Him; why would I have faith in Him?

We seek to come to know our Savior better in several ways. We pray together as a family morning and night. We daily study the Scriptures as a family. We sing hymns. We worship weekly on the Sabbath and renew our promises to Him. We seek to see His blessings in our lives and thank Him.

As we do these things, we come to know Him and feel His love. It isn't an instant knowledge, but one of faith, built over time.

Many of the above ideas are discussed as their own individual ingredients. I want to mention three here:

. . .

Study the Names and Titles of the Savior

One Christmas we picked a different name or title of the Savior to study each day in December. We discussed how He is our advocate and our healer, how He gathers us like a hen gathereth her chicks, etc.

Handel's Messiah *Oratorio*

A different Christmas, we studied the words from Handel's *Messiah* as we listened to the different sections. The combination of music and words helped us feel God's love and come to know Him better.

The Living Christ – Testimony of the Apostles

One of my favorite testimonies of our Savior is *The Living Christ*[1] given by His modern apostles. One year our family memorized *The Living Christ*. Since then, we've all forgotten the exact words, but phrases are still part of our family conversation.

~

Trust Christ

> I know that he loveth his children; nevertheless, I do not know the meaning of all things.
>
> —I Nephi 11:17

This is one of my favorite Scriptures. I don't know the reason hard things happen. I don't know if the pleadings of my heart will be answered in the way I hope. But I do know that my Savior loves me, and He loves all His children. I've felt His love, seen His love, and learned through experience that everything He does is with perfect love. (see my "Into the Oven" chapters for more on this).

When a child is going through a hard time or says that they feel that they'll never be good enough, we often turn to this Scripture to help them realize their worth and God's love for them. When we do this, they gain the confidence to move forward, trusting in the Lord.

We are slowly getting to the point where we can also say, "I know that God loveth His children. Even though I don't know the reason for what I'm going through, I'll trust and follow Him."

~

Put Him First

> And thou shalt love the Lord thy God with all thine heart, and with all thy soul, and with all thy might.
> —Deuteronomy 6:5

My day and my head are full of many things from the mundane "time to do laundry" to the emergency "my child needs stitches" to the exciting "this is such a cool story idea!" It is easy to get lost in the day-to-day. In other words, I'm easily distracted. And when I get distracted with less important things, it impacts how I act toward my Heavenly Father, my Savior, and my loved ones. When distracted, I only give them part of my attention, and I get annoyed and frustrated easily.

"The word *sin* in the New Testament comes from the Greek word *hamartia,* which means 'missing the mark'."

In archery, when a person is distracted—loses focus or is looking somewhere other than the target—he misses the target or mark. In life, a distraction doesn't need to be bad to cause us to miss the mark or path of the gospel; it just needs to get us to focus somewhere else.

This doesn't mean I can't have interests outside of the gospel. Our Savior wants us to develop our unique talents and to take joy in life. But I have to remember never to let those other interests take precedence over the most important things.

When I put God first in my life, everything starts to fall into the proper place or fall out of my life. I accomplish much more; my relationships are richer and more fulfilling; my whole life is more beautiful. Life isn't perfect, but it is much better.

. . .

Observations on Putting God First

Morning Joys

We wanted to help start out the day with the right focus, so we created our Morning Joys. They are: *pray, get dressed, make bed,* and *individually study Scriptures*. When we gather for breakfast, I ask, "did you do your morning joys?" Sometimes there is a groaning "of course" or "I forgot". Yet, it sets the tone for the day. When we forget in the rush of some mornings, we see the difference from not having started the day focused on our Lord.

Currently we have two sons who are learning to read. For individual Scripture study, one of them reads with me and the other reads with Pecan. It's only about five minutes. But those five minutes make a huge difference. I'm so grateful for Pecan's service to help his little brother feel the sweet spirit of the Lord's words.

Sabbath

I give one day in seven to focus on my Savior. I set aside all my writing, my projects, and the weekly tasks. I strive to consecrate my mind, my heart, and my soul to draw closer to Heavenly Father and Jesus Christ.

Then Monday comes and I accomplish more on Monday than any other day of the week. My mind is clearer, my emotions more level, my abilities enhanced. I love Mondays because of Sundays.

The same thing happens when I set aside time to serve others. I give up time, and the time remaining seems expanded.

Motherhood

I love creating stories. My first pen pal and I swapped stories in letters. I made up stories for my sisters at bedtime. I wrote my first novel in college.

When I entered motherhood, I found I didn't have the time or mental energy to write much. My writing became relegated to journal entries. I sacrificed my writing and consecrated my days to changing diapers, singing songs, tempering tantrums, reading out loud, home-schooling, seeking divine guidance, and welcoming additional children. These are joyful years.

Yet fourteen years later, when I again had the energy to write, I found that Heavenly Father had blessed me. All the years of experience, all the tender mercies and trials, life and God's blessings, combined to make my skill in writing and my ability to think so much more than they would have been if I stayed focused only in writing and never welcomed children into my life.

Note: I have many wonderful friends who haven't married or are unable to have children. They are putting our Savior first in other beautiful, equally important ways. Motherhood is only one of many ways to serve God.

~

Choose Faithful Obedience

A Family Discussion: Build upon the Rock

Therefore whosoever heareth these sayings of mine, and doeth them, I will liken him unto a wise man, which built his house upon a rock:

And the rain descended, and the floods came, and the winds blew, and beat upon that house; and it fell not: for it was founded upon a rock.

—Matthew 7:24-25

The Scriptures didn't say he "stood upon the rock" but he "built his house upon the rock". We must do more than just stand on the gospel; we must build our lives—our work, our families, our hobbies, all our focuses, all our leisure—on the rock of the gospel. It requires work. This work is active rather than passive, ongoing rather than a singular event.

When we've built a house, are we done and don't have to do anything more? No. A house, especially one subjected to storms, needs maintenance: shingles replaced, walls painted, windows weather-proofed, cracks patched. It takes daily, weekly, and yearly maintenance.

And so do we. We need to be continually maintaining our house on the rock of our Savior. We need daily prayer and Scripture study, weekly worship, renewing covenants, service. He is our sure foundation on which we daily build our lives.

~

POEMS OF PRAISE

About three years ago, I started writing poems about our Savior in December—sometimes focusing on one of His titles and other times on how He impacts my life.

Emmanuel – God is with us

The creator of the
heavens and the earth
didn't stay in the distant skies
to let us stumble on our way.

He came,
a helpless baby,
born in a stable
to a poor family.

He grew as a child,
in "wisdom and stature,
and in favour with God and man."

He walked the roads of Palestine,

ministering, teaching, healing.
He saw the publican in the tree.
He found the lame man
by the pool of Bethesda.

He suffered all things:
pain in body, mind, and spirit.
He felt every temptation
and bled in anguish,
yet never fell to wickedness.

Though perfect, He experienced
each of our imperfections,
each of our struggles;
so He knows how to succour us.

He paid for each of our sins,
suffering to the full extent of the law,
so we may be free to repent.

Emmanuel is no distant God.
He is with us.

—Inspired by Mosiah 3, Alma 7:11-13, Luke 2:52

Peace

Broken. Shattered.
Pieces scattered
along life's path.

No glue,
no needle and thread,

can mend.

Then He gathers the pieces,
sets them in a mosaic of slivered glass,
and spreads His grace overtop.
Mending what cannot be mended.
Healing what cannot be healed.
Granting peace.

Faith, Hope, and Charity

Faith *in* Christ
brings our thoughts
into focus.

We seek to know Him,
remembering Him
in all we do.

We trust Him,
knowing all He does
is for our good.

We obey Him,
seeking to keep His
commandments.

We put Him first,
centering our
lives around Him.

Hope *through* Christ
touches our hearts

to move forward.

Through His atonement
we hope for a chance to change,
a way to be clean.

Through His resurrection
we hope for eternal
life, love, and joy.

Through His love
we hope and find value,
even when all mock our worth.

Through Him
we hope and press onward,
even when all seems dark.

Charity *of* Christ
shows us God's love
in action.

He loves us with
time, focus, and gentleness—
the daily dedications.

He loves us with
patience and long suffering,
never giving up on us.

He loves us
even when we reject Him,
Beckoning us back.

He shows us love

and asks us to love one another
as He loves us.

—Inspired by Moroni 7

See more poems in Appendix: Poems of Praise.

INGREDIENT: PRAYER

"As soon as we learn the true relationship in which we stand toward God (namely, God is our Father, and we are His children), then at once prayer becomes natural and instinctive on our part (Matt. 7:7–11). ... The object of prayer is not to change the will of God but to secure for ourselves and for others blessings that God is already willing to grant but that are made conditional on our asking for them."
—Bible Dictionary

One year we decided to visit my little brother and his family in Connecticut. We had it all planned out, but April weather didn't agree with our plans. Or as the pilot said, "The doors have been secured. We are heading to Minneapolis. If that wasn't in your plans, well, your plans have now changed." We "enjoyed" a roller coaster ride of turbulence and skid-landed in a snow bound Minneapolis, where we stayed overnight because all outbound flights were canceled.

All night and into the morning, my parents, who we were traveling with, worked to get onto overbooked flights while keeping adults with children. Nana managed to get her, Pecan and Lime on standby for three different flights to Connecticut, each of them with multiple stops between.

When they arrived at the airport early in the morning, Nana asked the ticket agent if it were possible to get on a direct flight to Connecticut.

The agent said, "Impossible, it is already overbooked by eight, but I'll put you on standby for it." Nana and the boys sat down to wait and hope. The direct flight loaded and loaded. The ticket agent came over and said, "Well, you might get on, we are only overbooked by four."

Nana turned to Lime and Pecan and said, "Let's pray that we can get on." Lime immediately bowed his head, while Pecan went behind some chairs and knelt to pray. A short time later, their names were called to get on the overbooked plane.

Not all our prayers are answered like this. But it helped me see how much our Heavenly Father does hear us, and, when it is right in His wisdom, blesses us with the desired blessings.

~

I'd like to discuss four parts of prayer:

- Gratitude
- Repentance
- Seeking guidance
- Seeking blessings

~

GRATITUDE

Years ago, when our children were just little, we wanted to help them see with gratitude and fill their prayers with praise instead of just asking, so we started our pre-prayer "thankfuls".

Thankfuls

Thankful One

Before family prayer we each say one thankful.
Cherry's list extended for minutes:
dragonflies, homemade bread, wooden blocks, brothers...

"Cherry," I interrupted, "we need to pray."

"But I'm not done yet."

Thankful Two

"Thank Thee for
bread,
tuna,
relish,
mayo,
mustard,
lettuce,
but not celery."

Cherry prays over our tuna sandwiches.

Thankful Three

Pre-prayer thankfuls:
"Daddy, what are you thankful for?"

Pecan knows the answer.
"Daddy's thankful for Mommy."

A Child's Prayer

Cherry stepped on a bee.
"I burned my foot!"

Her skin stretches taut.

That night she prays,
"Thank you for helping my
foot get better.
Thank you for bumblebees,
even though they hurt.
I stepped on one
and burned my foot,
but I have a Band-Aid
and it is feeling better.
Thank you."

She spoke to a friend and Father.

~

REPENTANCE

I'm going to address repentance more in a different chapter, so I'll keep this brief. I make mistakes all the time. I get angry, frustrated, judgmental. I need the blessing of daily repentance. I need the time to talk with my Heavenly Father about what's been difficult, what I'm struggling with, and seek His help in changing and becoming better.

When I'm helping my children in this same process of change, prayer is an important step. Usually the more I talk, the less they hear. But when I ask them to go talk to Heavenly Father, they often are open to talking with me afterwards.

~

SEEKING GUIDANCE

Prayer isn't me speaking into a void, listing wishes. It is a two-way communication. However, hearing God's answers takes work and practice. I have to take time to study, find a quiet place to listen, and write down the thoughts and impressions that come, then act on them.

pray, listen, record, act
(thank, repeat)

Counsel with the Lord

Counsel with the Lord in all thy doings, and he will direct thee for good; yea, when thou liest down at night lie down unto the Lord, that he may watch over you in your sleep; and when thou risest in the morning let thy heart be full of thanks unto God; and if ye do these things, ye shall be lifted up at the last day.
—Alma 37:37

Journaled Thoughts from the Time of Four Children.

"Counsel with the Lord in all thy doings, and he will direct thee for good."

I am working on taking quiet time every morning, before the kids get up, to pray uninterrupted. It is fast becoming my "sweet hour of prayer." I find myself talking to my Heavenly Father, telling him what is happening in my life, in my family; my concerns and my desires. I also try to just listen, then write down the impressions I receive. As I counsel with my Heavenly Father, I feel at peace. I don't know what will happen, but I do know that He is in control and loves me, and He will support me with whatever trials come (and they will come). More and more often, what I pray for is changes in myself instead of changes of circumstances.

"When thou liest down at night, lie down unto the Lord."

When I go to bed, I again try to take a quiet time (not nearly as long as the morning, but still unhurried) to pray. I thank my Heavenly Father for his many, specific blessings this day. I tell him all that is happening, pray for those around me, and again pray for help. Once I've unloaded my problems, most often I am able to go to sleep with peace. I'm able to let things go, knowing they are in good hands—God's hands.

"When thou risest in the morning, let thy heart be full of thanks unto God."

For about a week, I've tried to keep my morning prayers as ones only of gratitude. This is proving an interesting challenge, since this is also my uninterrupted prayer time and when I talk about all my concerns, counsel with the Lord, and plead for help. But as I focus on gratitude for God's many, many blessings and bring all I have before him in the light of gratitude (even my concerns and pleadings), I am buoyed up for the day. I feel so optimistic because I've just realized again how many blessings I have. I also feel humbled. Seeing all that God has blessed me with is a good check on pride and selfishness.

A family Discussion: How Do You Hear Him?

After prayer, my young son asked, "Did you hear him answer?"

"Who?" I asked.

"The person you were talking to—Heavenly Father."

It is an important question.

We asked in our family, "How do you hear our Savior?"

- My husband: I know it's from God when the thought or idea comes fully formed in simplicity and clarity. I usually have to slowly piece together the idea (as do most of us).
- Me: Usually it comes as a thought or impression to do something specific. And when I write down the thought and act on it, I receive more such thoughts and impressions. It's

never a feeling of fear. God never speaks by fear, so that is a good test. Even His warnings are cautions without fear.

- Cherry: I often feel the Spirit through music.
- Pecan: I don't really know when I hear Him. (So we talked about how he may hear God's direction in his thoughts, because Pecan often says profound things.)
- Apple: I feel Him through family time together.
- Lime: He feels like a good feeling. I feel Him in hugs.
- Huckleberry: I feel Him in quiet times. (He's my most energetic child—so this was an interesting comment, and a sweet one.)
- Strawberry: She didn't take part in the conversation (she was three years old), but later she showed me a wooden block building she made. "There's the temple." She pointed to a big block in the middle of it. "There's Jesus." Then she pointed to a block right next to the Jesus block. "That's me."

Followup question: "What can we do to hear Him better?"

- Remove distractions.
- Pray every day.
- Ponder, take time to reflect.
- Hold to what we know is true.
- Live the gospel and commandments.
- Act on inspiration quickly and with exactness.
- Share our testimony of our Savior with others.

Finding a Quiet Place

Behold, who art thou, that thou shouldst be afraid of man, who shall die, and of the son of man, who shall be made like unto grass? And

forgettest the Lord thy maker, that hath stretched forth the heavens, and laid the foundations of the earth...
—2 Nephi 8:12-13

Why do people tend to fear or give attention to men instead of God? My husband replied, "Because the things of the world are right in front of us—demanding our attention."

It's like having the TV on in a room. Everyone ends up looking at it even if it isn't that interesting. It takes turning off the TV or leaving the room to be able to focus on other things again. It's like that with Heavenly Father too. We sometimes have to get away from the world to be able to focus.

Distractions

My biggest distractions
are not
others,
they are
myself.

My thoughts run like
trains through Central Station.
Express and freight, criss crossing:
God, husband, children, writing,
homeschool, laundry, meals, service.

Multiple lines at once,
and all too often hijacked.
I start my prayer,
"Dear Heavenly Father"
Only for thoughts to flit off,
Did I turn off the stove?

I begin reading Scriptures:
"And it came to pass,"
and ten verses pass
before I realize my thoughts
have taken a scenic tour of a
book I'm writing.

So I refocus.
I start again.
I pray for help with my
own distractedness.

Let's Go Look it Up

Growing up, most often when I asked my dad a question, he'd answer by saying, "Let's go look it up," even though most times I'm sure he already knew the answer.

I realized that Heavenly Father's answer to so many of my questions is, "Let's go look it up." He answers through the Scriptures or words of the modern prophets, and sometimes through other good books. He doesn't expect me to do it alone, but He answers my question through both the words read and the impressions to my mind and heart. He is in effect saying, "Let's go look it up. I'll help you find the answer," because though He knows all things, He also knows that I will remember it better if I have to do some work.

Initiative and Revelation

But, behold, I say unto you, that you must study it out in your mind; then you must ask me if it be right, and if it is right I will cause that your bosom shall burn within you; therefore, you shall feel that it is right.
—Doctrine and Covenants 9:8

We are to seek to do good of our own free will and seek guidance as we move forward, instead of waiting to be commanded in all things. As often as not, the instruction I receive is a warm feeling of comfort that Heavenly Father is pleased with the direction I'm going.

It's like my child checking in with me as they learn a new skill. Sometimes I give further pointers, but often I just cheer them on. In their process of figuring things out, they learn the skill better than if I directed every single step—and sometimes they discover new ways to do it that I didn't even know. (Of course that isn't the case with God; He knows all the ways, which makes it all the more wonderful that He lets us work things out).

Hearing Him Helps Prevent Burnout

> And see that all these things are done in wisdom and order; for it is not requisite that a man should run faster than he has strength. And again, it is expedient that he should be diligent, that thereby he might win the prize; therefore, all things must be done in order.
> —Mosiah 4:27

I'm a mother, wife, daughter, sister, friend, and writer. I carry many roles. There is too much in any day for me to accomplish all that I could do. I need the sweet peace and direction of the Comforter. I need personal revelation to know what to focus on and when. It is impossible and unnecessary to do it all at once. I strive to determine through daily prayer, study, and listening what parts to work on today, and then again the next day. These guiding steps help me stay balanced and healthy, and able to grow closer to my Savior.

Don't Judge if Someone Receives Different Instruction from Me

Mosiah 22:12 and 23:1 What Limhi's people brought versus Alma's people when they fled captivity.

- Limhi's people brought gold, silver, all precious things, and provisions.
- Alma's people brought flocks and grain

At first I thought Alma's people were much wiser, but maybe they both were inspired for their specific situation. Alma's people went to an uninhabited land and had to establish farms. The flocks and grain allowed them to do so. Limhi's people traveled to a city, and their precious things could have allowed them to purchase land and supplies and get established that way.

I need to be careful not to judge another because they receive a different personal revelation than I do.

A Lesson from my Child: Listening to the Holy Ghost

We lost the key to our shed that held all our chicken food and supplies. We started a frantic search through the kids' jackets and around the garage. Then we started searching through the toys and the kids' clothes.

Both my husband and I felt stressed because of the cost of getting the lock picked or cut. Then I remembered that we needed to calm down and come together for family prayer. Jesse asked me to say the prayer, and I prayed that Heavenly Father would guide us to where the key was and help us to listen so we could hear the promptings of the Holy Ghost.

After prayer, we went in different directions to search again. I worked beside Pecan, looking through toys, and then went to check on Cherry. She was going through all the pockets of her clothes (she was the last one to have the key). She stopped every once in a while and just stood there. The first time she did this, I reminded her to keep looking, and she gently told me, "Mom, I'm listening."

After we'd gone through all her clothes and looked under her and her sister's beds and in the toys and in drawers, I told her to go back upstairs, because we had looked everywhere in her bedroom.

She said, "Mom, I feel that they are close by. I want to keep looking here."

I swallowed my words, humbled by her faith, "I'm glad you are listening. You keep looking here."

I went into the bathroom next to her bedroom to look—a place I hadn't thought to look before. I saw some hair things peeking out from under the sink, on the floor. I bent down to pick them up, and there were the keys. I'm so grateful my daughter continued to listen to the Holy Ghost even when I directed her to go someplace else, and that she told me what she was feeling.

~

SEEKING BLESSINGS

Every answered prayer is a miracle, because each is a divine intervention in our lives (see Moroni 7).

As our circle of family and friends expands, so do our prayers. We keep a list on our whiteboard of specific people, so we can remember them in our prayers. We also have a place on the whiteboard where we can each write our own prayer requests, so we can know what we can pray specifically for each other. These have included: *find a good friend, learn to enjoy science, be calm when frustrated, productive day at work,* and *toddler sleep better.*

Answering Prayers

As we pray for each other, Heavenly Father teaches us how to help. Sometimes it means a quick note of encouragement or a phone call. Sometimes it involves brainstorming together. Sometimes it means going and helping with manual labor. And sometimes the best way to help is further prayer. God helps us act as His hands in answering prayers.

Answered Prayers

I have to be careful, because sometimes I fall into feeling that if I pray hard enough, the desired blessing will happen. But I'm continually reminded that though God always answers prayers, the answers seem to come in three types: *yes, not yet,* or *I have something better in store for you.* The answer is always the best one for me and given with love, even if it isn't the one I hoped for.

No *and* Not Yet *Answers*

Strawberry asked me for a treat, and I told her she needed to finish her lunch first. So she asked Pecan for the same thing. He said, "Go ask Mommy."

She replied, "I did, and she didn't answer."

I repeated my answer so both she and Pecan could hear, and Pecan said, "Mommy gave you a no answer."

Strawberry pouted, "But I wanted a *yes* answer."

I wonder how many times I think Heavenly Father didn't answer my prayers because I didn't get the *yes* answer I was hoping for? His *no* answer is still given with love, even if it isn't what I wanted. And sometimes it isn't a no, but rather, *not yet* or *this needs to happen first.*

I need to be careful not to seek someone else to give me what I want, when God has clearly given me a *no* or *not yet* answer. Trying to undermine or get around His will always leads to grief.

Though if the answer is not clearly a no, then I feel it is right and expected to continue to seek desired blessings and to not grow weary in prayer.

Consecrate Performance

> But behold, I say unto you that ye must pray always, and not faint; that ye must not perform any thing unto the Lord save in the first place ye shall pray unto the Father in the name of Christ, that he will

consecrate thy performance unto thee, that thy performance may be for the welfare of thy soul.

—2 Nephi 32:9

I try to pray to Heavenly Father that he will consecrate my "performance" unto me and that it will be for the welfare of my soul. It doesn't say my "success," but rather my actions. It is my experiences and my choices that change me and help me grow to be like Him. Not necessarily the results of my endeavors.

∼

Attention Span and Family Prayers

As we've implemented many of the above ideas into family prayers, the prayers have grown longer and longer. One time I was praying, and Strawberry decided it had gone on long enough and ended the prayer for me.

So in an attempt to remember all those we are praying for and to express real gratitude in our prayers, we decided in a Family Council to focus our morning family prayers on those who need blessings and help, and focus our evening family prayers on gratitude. I'm grateful for this inspiration to meet the attention spans of our little, and not so little, ones.

I hope our children's individual prayers still have a good balance of both.

INGREDIENT: SCRIPTURE STUDY

> My soul delighteth in the Scriptures, and my heart pondereth them, and writeth them for the learning and the profit of my children. Behold, my soul delighteth in the things of the Lord; and my heart pondereth continually upon the things which I have seen and heard.
> —2 Nephi 4:15

Let me describe a typical family Scripture study.

We read the Scriptures at breakfast time—because we have a semi-captive audience. Verses are interspersed with "please pass the water" and "guess what I dreamed last night." Our youngest ones are usually running around making loud noises. We rarely get through a whole chapter.

This may sound familiar. Do you ever wonder, "Why do we do this—is anyone listening—does it make any difference?"

It is worth it. And it can be a delight.

~

How to Feast upon the Scriptures

I think there must be as many ways to learn from the Scriptures as there are people. These are some of my favorite ways.

1. Look for How the Scriptures testify of Christ

The Old Testament testifies of Jehovah. The New Testament testifies of Christ. The Book of Mormon is another testament of Jesus Christ. The Doctrine and Covenants is filled with His words. Each book of Scripture teaches us who He is, how He loves us, and how to follow Him.

2. Conversation About What We are Reading in an Informal Setting

Remember the noisy breakfast-time picture, with interrupted Scripture reading. Interspersed are delightful conversations on something we read. I love the discussions and the discoveries.

Some are funny. When we were reading Genesis 22:17, our oldest son said, "Sandwiches upon the seashore! It said sandwiches!" I looked back through the verse and saw what he heard. It says "and as the sand which is upon the seashore." I will probably never hear that part of the Abrahamic Covenant the same way again.

Another time my husband started reading Laman and Lemual's murmuring in the voices of Statler and Waldorf, the Muppet hecklers.

Some discussions are profound. We were talking about repentance and how some people look at sin with the idea of "I can always repent," and use that to excuse willful sin. Our oldest son said, "It's like saying I can always heal, then jump off the roof of a house". Which led to a long discussion on the work of repentance being like the work of physical therapy for an injury.

A different discussion centered around the difference between sacrifice and consecration.

3. Notebook and Pen

> For it were not possible that our father, Lehi, could have remembered
> all these things, to have taught them to his children, except it were for
> the help of these plates. —Mosiah 1:4

The pen is mightier than the sword, or in my case, than my memory. I have to capture things quickly on paper or they slip away. Mommy brain, and I'm grateful for it. Because of the need to write things down for short-term memory, I also have a long-term record that I can study later.

I don't have any color-coded marking system or organized method of study. I like to jot down thoughts and ideas, then maybe ponder on them throughout the day and perhaps even bring them up at dinner time. I don't record scripture thoughts daily, but when I take the time to do this, Heavenly Father teaches me.

4. Ask Questions

Asking questions is a wonderful way to learn from the Scriptures. For example:

Whose law are we living?

> For I say unto you, That except your righteousness shall exceed the
> righteousness of the scribes and Pharisees, ye shall in no case enter
> into the kingdom of heaven.
> —Matthew 5:20

The Pharisees lived a very strict law of outward righteousness focused on themselves—they had faith in themselves and not God. Jesus calls us to live a law of faith focused on Him and obedience to Him, not our own created laws. And it is a much more forgiving and freeing way to live. Whose law are we living?

· · ·

5. Apply in Life

Peace, be still.
—Mark 4:39

There is a difference between being anxiously engaged in good works and frantically engaged. I cannot imagine the Savior running from one thing to the next, always thinking of a long list of good things He needs to get done (though I've fallen into that mode myself plenty of times).

He went about doing good, lifting others one by one, being completely present with the person He was serving at the time. And no, His life wasn't surrounded by calm. Remember the friends who lowered a crippled man down through the roof, because they couldn't get him to Jesus any other way. If anyone was constantly beset by pressure and demands, it was our Savior, yet He took the time to individually minister to the one, and He took time to renew Himself through prayer.

And when he had sent the multitudes away, he went up into a mountain apart to pray: and when the evening was come, he was there alone.
—Matthew 14:23

Sometimes we may feel the way He did, with the clamor of multiple children demanding our attention at the same time or the clamor of the task list that never ends.

What happens when we take the time to quietly ponder a Scripture, praying at the beginning or end of the day when all is quiet? When all the children are in bed and the computer and TV are turned off? What happens when we quietly ponder our Savior's life and His gift?

6. Intensive Study
Mosiah 28:10—29:1

King Mosiah had no one to confer the kingdom upon; his sons had all refused. The very next thing he did wasn't to work on that problem directly. Instead, he studied all the Scriptures—plates of brass and plates of Nephi, and he translated the plates of Ether and studied them too.

It is only after this massive study of Scripture that he set up a new government, one ruled by judges.

Sometimes to receive the guidance we desire, we need to put in intensive time studying God's word.

~

Family Scripture Laughs

Over the years we've enjoyed many wonderful misreadings and misunderstandings in family Scriptures. Here are some of our favorites.

A child asked, "What do provisions mean?"

"Provisions mean food and clothing."

"Oh, food and loathing."

A daughter read "...ye need not suppose that the righteous are lost because they are slain; but behold, they do enter into the rest of the Lord their God." (Alma 60:13) However, it sounded like, "ye need not suppose that the righteous are lost because they are *insane.*"

Another daughter asked, "Are babies born with germs?"

I replied, "No."

"How do they get them?"

"From other people."

"Then how did Adam get them?"

. . .

A child read, "The carcasses were mangled by dogs and wild *beets* of the wilderness" instead of "wild beasts". (Alma 16:10)

And of course the "sandwiches upon the seashore" (Genesis 22:17)

~

Family Scripture Study Discussions and Games

Our family Scripture study often turns into discussions and occasional games. Here are two of them.

Armor of God

> *Put on the whole armour of God...*
> —*Ephesians 6:11*

As we studied Ephesians 6, we discussed each piece of armor, the part of the body it protected, and how that protected us spiritually. This is the table we came up with:

Piece of Armor	Part of Body Protected	Body Represents Spiritually	How the Armor Protects
loins girt with truth	loins	virtue, potential for posterity	Truth helps us keep our virtue; to know the importance and value of family and intimate relationships.
breastplate of righteousness	heart	passions, desires, emotions	Knowing right from wrong helps us bridle our passions and keep them within God's bounds.
feet shod with the preparation of the gospel of peace	feet	direction/path in life	Covenant path. As we walk this path, we will have peace now and in the eternities. Leads to peace.
shield of faith	front of body	additional protection from multiple directions	Faith gives protection where we are weak. It helps protect all the other areas: heart, mind, loins, etc.
helmet of salvation	head	thoughts	Knowing God's plan for His children gives us perspective. It helps us make wise decisions that impact us eternally. Also salvation comes through our Savior and His atonement. Our thoughts are always to be directed toward Him.
sword of God's Spirit	active, attack	drives away the bad, helps protect others	When we act on promptings from the Spirit we are taking action. We can drive off evil and protect others.

A Family Activity: Heart of Clay

For God maketh my heart soft...
   —Job 23:16

I handed each person a small cube of clay and asked them to make a heart.

Our hearts are like clay.

We need spiritual waters to keep our heart soft and changeable. Life with all its frustrations, stresses, and expectations dries us out and makes us harder of heart.

But if we rehydrate with spiritual waters of (these are the ones we came up with in our family): Scriptures, church, prayer, listening to the prophet, heeding the Holy Ghost, attending the temple, sacrament, wholesome recreational activities, and forgiveness, we will have a softened heart and be able to change to be better and more like Heavenly Father and our Savior.

A hard heart is dried out. When we applied water to dry-ish clay it took a lot of work to knead that moisture through and make the clay soft again. At first the water just sat on the surface. Likewise, if we dehydrate from spiritual waters it will take work and time to get a soft heart again. But with the Savior's atonement it is never too late to become soft hearted, no matter how dried out and hard we become.

Even if we are doing pretty well in our life, if we stop partaking of daily spiritual waters, we will become brittle, and the storms of life will break us.

INGREDIENT: GRATITUDE

Years ago, a friend wrote to me, "You never complain."

I responded, "Ha! You can't hear my thoughts. I try to stop the complaints there. It is a lifelong learning process and I hope someday the complaints won't even happen there. My best tool for it is to find three 'gratefuls' and focus on those instead. It helps me change my attitude."

Well the complaints in my thoughts haven't stopped; I'm still working on that. But I've learned much through the following exercise of three "gratefuls"/three compliments.

> "What would happen if the next time you feel like complaining, you first state out loud three 'gratefuls' specific to the situation? What would happen if the next time you feel like criticizing someone, you first express three compliments to them?"[1]

In expansion of that practice, several years ago I decided to write a thankful poem each day in November. I specifically picked topics that I felt tempted to complain about: noise, clutter, auto trouble, health issues, etc. Then I worked to find God's blessings in each of these situations and put it into poetry.

I still struggle with the same things that I've written about in gratitude. I still have a difficult time with the constant noise of nurturing six growing children. I still have to take deep breaths when a child is tantruming. I still have to repent of yelling and harsh words. Health challenges have not gone away. But I have hope and joy in seeing God's many tender mercies, and little by little I am growing closer to Him.

Grateful in All Things

God's apostle spoke
difficult and comforting words:
Be grateful in all things.

Not for, but in.

My "grateful for" list is
never-ending, when I start it:
family, home, food,
earth's beauty, health,
stories, learning, creating.

Never-ending,
but each one endable.

Could I lose each of those,
like the Christian martyrs
or the Jews in Holocaust,
and still be grateful?

There is one sure and eternal
focal point of gratitude:
My Savior.

And as I am grateful to

Him, my
Creator,
Redeemer, and
Advocate,

I learn to be grateful
in all things, both
beautiful and difficult.

And my life, which is
filled to overflowing with
blessings, increases in
richness of
understanding and joy.

—inspired by Dieter F. Uchtdorf[2] and Betsy Ten Boom[3]

Gratitude and Humor

Sometimes I feel grinchy and want to complain. One day a child was in that mindset. I said, "Take a deep breath and..." She scowled as I paused. Then I said, "stand on your head and yell, 'Chicken!'" Her scowl morphed into laughter. When she could stop laughing she said, "I thought you were going to tell me to say three 'gratefuls.'"

Sometimes humor is the gateway into gratitude.

Gratitude and Honesty

Seeing blessings doesn't mean ignoring problems. We council as a family each week on difficulties and brainstorm solutions. We have individual interviews with our kids, and one of the questions is, "What is difficult?" It is important to address those areas.

~

LEMONADE POEMS

"Prevent murmuring by replacing the complaints with seeing God's blessings and seeking his help."
  —*heard in church*

A selection of my November lemonade poems, finding the sweetness in the difficult or mundane parts of life.

Interruptions

My life is made of—
"Mommy, look at this"—
broken moments of time.

A Scripture caught between—
"He hit me"—
efforts of patience.

Writing fractured into—
"I'm hungry"—
half sentences.

Children are not—
"Will you please let me finish"—
interruptions.

They are the
Focus of my life.

The Noisy Hours

6 a.m. My toddler wakes and
pounds on the door,
soon followed by my five-year-old
and four others.

From that moment, until each child is
snug in bed, I am in an ocean of noise.
Voices
beating against me,
washing over me, sometimes making it
hard to breathe.

I'm not good with noise.
Ironic, considering that as a child, my
voice carried three houses over.
My children have my robust lungs.

Yet if I can listen beyond the noise, I find
laughter growing from geeky jokes, funny faces;
pretending, exploring worlds that only live in the mind;
singing, off key and full of heart;
thumping feet of healthy, rambunctious children;
constant voiced "Mommy",
letting me know I'm needed and loved.

Even the spats between siblings,
tantrums, and complaints are
blessed noises, because they remind me to
teach my children in a better way.

Patience. Daily lessons in patience.
And a yard, where children can play loudly.

A fisherman faces the sea each day
to provide for his family.
I face a sea of noise each day
to nurture mine.

Creative Clutter

Creative clutter
speckles the house on some days,
engulfs it on others.

Books pile high on every horizontal surface,
stick out between couch cushions,
saved for later when called to lunch.

Scraps of papers,
remnants of projects,
show a trail to the creative party.

Tower of Babel block towers
totter on carpet bases.

Couch cushions and blankets turn into caves and forts.
Encyclopedias' weighty knowledge holds down the blanket
    corners that
span the room in technicolored tents.

Dress-up box empty,
children pretend ninjas, knights, fairies, and reindeer.
Moment-ago costumes pile in the corners.

Muddy boots,

dripping from romps through rain-soaked fields,
lie by the door next to raincoats and cast-off mittens.

Stuffed animals sag in a tea-party circle
around dented metal play dishes.
The toddler carefully feeds each one.

Just before dinner, the children will go through the house,
in a whirlwind of reverse chaos,
putting away, cleaning up, straightening.

And at the end of it
books will pile haphazardly on the shelves,
clay dragons will stare from high surfaces,
new drawings will replace old on the fridge.

And memories will be tucked away,
to be pulled out again for future generations.

Cook and Eat and Wash

Cook and Eat and Wash.
Day in, day out.
Cook the meals.
Eat the food.
Wash the dishes.

Cook and Eat and Wash.
Week in, week out.
Chop the veggies.
Bear the refusal.
Wash away the residue.

Cook and Eat and Wash.
Year in, year out.
Friendships grown preparing.
Lives shared over food.
Service learned cleaning.

Cook and Eat and Wash.
Three daily parts of
nurturing my
Family.

Expedition

Clad in Christopher Robin
red rubber rain boots,
my five-year-old picks
birthday gifts for his best friends.

A quick trip to the store and back.
Or it should be.
I turn the key and van trills clicks.

"Mommy, what's wrong?"

"Let's pray and ask
Heavenly Father's help."

We pray.
More trilling clicks.
I can't find my phone.

There's a lube shop down the street.

The sun is bright and the
autumn air crisp.

He skips alongside me,
happily chattering,
"It's so sad the van is broken."

"But we are on an expedition,
Just like Christopher Robin."

"Yes, an adventure!"

The lube shop says,
"Sounds like a broken starter.
Sorry, can't help.
But there's a mechanic shop not far."

Pointed in a new direction,
we race each other down the sidewalk.

The mechanic listens to our tale,
"Probably battery. Let's try a
jump start."

It works!
We drive to the mechanic shop
and get a new battery,
because the old was shot.

My little boy chatters while we wait,
"We prayed, but the van didn't work
until you helped."

I respond as the mechanic listens,
"Sometimes Heavenly Father answers prayers

by telling us to go look for help."

They check everything else out
to make sure nothing else was
causing a problem.

The bill they print only
shows charge for the
battery and installation.

Angels in grease-stained coveralls,
and a little boy with a
flair for adventure.

Blessing of a Headache

I do not like headaches,
I do not like them, Sam-I-am.

I do not like them in the night.
I do not like them with all my might.
I do not like them in the day.
I do not like them in any way.

But the ache is rare,
The message clear.
The pounding knock
upon my head.

Hark, listen, hear me now,
Slow down, sleep more, and careful tread.
Your body's fighting hard.
Rest, and then I'll stop the

rapping that you dread.

First Words

My child's first word:
"Mama."

And some days,
even years later,
feels like his only word.

I'm hungry,
"Mom!"
I need help,
"Mommy!"
Watch this,
"Mom!"

The call comes when
my hands are full,
my thoughts occupied,
my emotions ragged

yelled past others,
willing to help
but invisible to him.

He is a lesson in
childlike faith.
Do I turn to God with such
single-minded focus?

And even as I

teach him to temper
his voice and
see who else can help,
I try to learn to
turn my pleas heavenward
with the same zeal.

INGREDIENT: FREEDOM

Wherefore, men are free according to the flesh; and all things are given them which are expedient unto man. And they are free to choose liberty and eternal life, through the great Mediator of all men, or to choose captivity and death, according to the captivity and power of the devil; for he seeketh that all men might be miserable like unto himself.
—2 Nephi 2:27

I'm a bit of a stubborn person. If someone explains and then lets me choose, then I'm open to listening. But I strongly dislike being pushed to do things. My children are the same. Especially Cherry. The more I push, the more she digs in her heels. I'm grateful she has this attribute. She is resilient against the trends of the world and the expectations of society.

I believe Heavenly Father wants us to choose instead of blindly follow. He doesn't push us. Instead He teaches us, shows us, and allows us to choose.

What is freedom?

My kids' history lesson asked them to write an idea related to freedom for each letter of the word.

. . .

Cherry's:

- Free to choose
- Responsible with your choices
- Everyone can help themselves safely
- Educated in the consequences of your choices
- Do the right and you will be more free
- Opening new possibilities
- Make your own decisions

Pecan's:

- Feelings and thoughts free
- Responsible in learning and for choices
- Education
- Endure through mistakes and hard things
- Do right
- Obey the law
- Merciful (those who forgive will receive forgiveness)

That evening we discussed freedom as a family.

What is freedom? Is it to get to do whatever you want? Is it life without restraints?

We defined freedom in three parts: Choice, Knowledge, Responsibility.

Choice: We need the power and freedom to choose, without compulsion.

- This is the one most people think of. God won't compel us. He will never use His power to make us change. It is always our choice.
- Others may try to compel us. Yet, in the darkest situations— like a WWII concentration camp—we see those who maintain their power to choose, even if the only thing they have power over is their attitude and how they treat others.

Knowledge: We need to know and understand the consequences, so we can make choices that lead to the desired consequences.

- Every action has a consequence for good or bad. Touching a hot stove has the consequence of a burn. Exercising has the consequence of better health. If I want a desired blessing or to avoid a specific struggle, I'd do well to study what leads to that situation.
- That doesn't mean I can avoid all trials or gain all blessings in this mortal life, but I'll be pointed in the right direction, and I'll grow closer to God our Law Giver and come to understand His loving direction.

Responsibility: Responsible for choices, both to act or not to act. Responsible for self.

- We can't be free if we don't take responsibility for our choices, or if we blame another for our choices. When we blame another, we are giving control over to someone else and lose a measure of our freedom.

Freedom is not boundless. Looking at science, we have the bounds of gravity, amongst many others. Removing gravity wouldn't make us more free, but rather make many actions much more difficult. Consider the difficulties astronauts have in space. But as we learn the laws of flight, then we can use gravity, lift and other laws to gain greater freedom of travel. It is the same with God's laws. Our freedom is expanded as we humbly expand our knowledge and live according to the knowledge gained.

Freedom is vital. I want to teach my children and then let them make their own decisions. I want them to grow strong in studying out situations, seeking God's guidance, and making wise choices.

∼

Law Giver

God gives us the
power to choose.
All the elements obey Him,
but we choose to obey or not.
He allowed a third of His children,
to lose their first estate,
rather than remove their choice.

God gives us knowledge:
what our choices are,
what consequences follow.
Prophet by prophet,
Scripture by Scripture,
He gives us the law,
showing us paths
and where they lead.

God gives us responsibility.
We go through life
building experiences,
bearing consequences,
metamorphosing.
And when we stand
in His presence again,
He will not take away

who we've become.

He gives us the Law
to help us return,
to show us the path,
the cliffs, the sinkholes.
It is through our Savior
and following in His way
we can become divine.

—Inspired by Doctrine and Covenants 29:36

~

Proper Authority

A common conflict is over one sibling not liking what another sibling is doing, and then trying to force the other sibling to change. We keep working on patience and asking calmly, and coming to a parent if something really needs to change. We came up with something we are calling the "Two Steps".

- Talk to the person calmly.
- If they don't listen, then either: let it go *or* go to a parent to address the issue.

We are trying to help them understand that they can't take the law into their own hands, that they should try to communicate calmly, but if the other person isn't listening, then they must go to the one in authority over the other person (parents, church leader, police, government). The exception is if someone is going to get hurt—then do physically intervene, and then go to an authority as soon as possible.

I can also do the "Two Steps" by talking to a child calmly, and if they are not calm, to send them to a calm place until they are ready to communicate, and while they are there I go to Heavenly Father in prayer.

～

Lord Omnipotent

Powerful enough to
move mountains
and change the
course of rivers

yet He will never force
the mind to move
nor change the course
of a heart's desire.

He beckons, teaches, loves.
He sends trials for our sake,
to help us see, to change.
But always we choose.

The Almighty God
gives us power over ourselves.
And when we've learned
the self-control to follow Him,
then we have moved something
mightier than mountains
—our hearts.

INGREDIENT: HONESTY

Providing for honest things, not only in the sight of the Lord, but also in the sight of men.
    —2 Corinthians 8:21

When my sixth child was a baby and I was getting up to nurse her in the middle of the night, I had a difficult time staying out of the ice cream. One day Jesse asked who was eating all the ice cream, and I sheepishly told him. He listened as I justified my actions and then as I admitted that it also made my eczema worse. He continued to quietly listen even after I stopped talking. In the silence, I asked him for help in figuring a way to stay out of the ice cream. After discussing several ideas, we decided to stick the ice cream in the garage freezer because it put it at a distance. The solution worked.

I know this is a silly example, but the same process of honesty, listening without judging, and then brainstorming together has helped in more serious situations.

∾

Honesty is vital in our family. When we are honest with each other, we trust each other, we can talk about anything, and we can help each other.

When we lack honesty, then hurts get buried and canker, bad habits cement, and trust dissolves.

When a child was struggling with honesty, we made the following gradient of honesty, from best- to worst-case scenario.

1. Tell the truth without a reminder.
2. Tell the truth when asked.
3. Lie, then later tell the truth.
4. Get caught in the lie.
5. Never get caught and never admit.

Never get caught and never admit is the worst-case scenario, because the lie festers and the person builds a habit of lying.

Home the Safest Place to make a Mistake

We want our home to be the safest place to make mistakes and to be honest. See the next section (Ingredient: Repentance) for more specifics on this.

To help in telling the truth, we make the consequence for an action less if admitted and more if lied about. We praise a child for telling the truth, even if they are in trouble.

Over time our children who have struggled with honesty are much more likely to tell the truth. Sometimes the truth comes out after many days. We've gotten notes slipped under our bedroom door from a child. Those are the sweetest notes. And the conversations afterwards are even sweeter.

Talk about Anything

We interview our children regularly, and one of the questions is,

"What is difficult?" When a child says nothing is difficult, I know that I need to pay more attention and build more trust.

For example, near the beginning of a son's second-grade year (this was our first year doing public school), he told me that some kids in his school were teasing and swearing at him. After hugs and thanking him for telling us, we brainstormed what we could do about the situation. We kept him in our prayers (including our family prayers) and kept checking back on the situation. I'm so grateful he came and told us.

Another time a child said that she didn't want to do more art lessons because she didn't like the drive. She is a talented artist and at first I wanted to persuade her to keep taking lessons. But (with a little nudge from God) I listened and then talked with Jesse about it. We stopped the lessons. She took other art lessons later on, but it was important that we listened to her honest sharing of how she was feeling.

We've told our children that when they see pornography (because this world is filled with it) that they should tell us. We've also told them if someone ever tells them not to tell us something, then to tell us immediately. So far it's only happened a few times, but we are grateful they've come and told us when it's happened.

INGREDIENT: COVENANTS

"A covenant is a sacred agreement between God and a person or group of people. God sets specific conditions, and He promises to bless us as we obey those conditions. When we choose not to keep covenants, we cannot receive the blessings, and in some instances we suffer a penalty as a consequence of our disobedience."[1]

Every year we drive 750 miles to visit family. The trip takes about thirteen hours. Cherry gets carsick every time. One year we had a flat tire going there and another one coming home. Boredom creeps in, followed by teasing and whining. We prepare the best we can with audio books, coloring pages, movies, games, songs, snacks for those who aren't carsick, and prayer. The trip is often arduous. But in the end, we see our family, and it is all worth it.

Life is a bit like that trip, and God's grace is like the vehicle. Our Savior and His atonement provide the vehicle for us to get back to our heavenly family, but unless we turn to and follow Him (like getting in the van and driving) we'll never get there. It is our effort to press forward on the path with all its trials, boredoms, and disappointments that keeps us going in the right direction, but without our Savior we'd never make it. He is the one who carries us.

Like on the family trip, on the path back to heaven:

- We have to follow the map to get there and not get sidetracked.
- We have to refuel spiritually along the way.
- We have to be patient in confined spaces and situations.
- Sometimes illness (like car sickness) or other trials hit, and we have to rearrange our plans, help the one hurting, and be patient as we continue our journey.
- We have to endure, because we really won't get there any sooner than we do.
- If we abandon our Savior (like abandoning the vehicle) because we just can't take the trip anymore, we won't make it.
- If we just sat at home and complained and wished to get there, it wouldn't do a single thing.
- Life has a lot more pleasant periods along the way than a 13-hour car trip. But either way, the end is so worth the journey!

It is true we could always walk. But unlike walking and eventually getting to see family, without our Savior we would never make it back to heaven.

But what does this have to do with covenants? Covenants are the path we travel as we follow our Savior.

When Jesse and I were children, we both made a covenant at baptism to follow Christ and put Him first. We renew that covenant each Sabbath. Our family started with the covenant of marriage before God. We help our children to also make covenants with God, walk His path, and receive the blessings that He seeks to give.

Here are a couple ways that we've discussed covenants in our family.

Analogy of the Mortgage

When we bought our house, we took out a mortgage. In our day and age, it is nearly impossible to buy a house outright, so we signed a contract saying we will pay on the debt of the house each month, and we get the privilege of living in it.

Baptism is similar in that we have a debt that we cannot pay on our own, and Heavenly Father has blessings He wants to give us, but those specific blessings require a covenant.

Our Savior paid our debt. He asks us to covenant and "pay" our (infinitesimally small) part by keeping His commandments, repenting, and trying to do a little better each day.

In exchange we get the blessings that allow us to grow closer to Him and receive all that He has.

Parable of the Apprenticeship

A man wanted to become a carpenter. He dreamed about it. He talked about it with his friends. He tried to shape wood. He did everything he could. But his skill wasn't much.

One day a master carpenter saw his attempts and offered to take him as an apprentice. The man was ecstatic. He signed the apprenticeship contract. Every day, he came, he listened, he focused, and he worked. And little by little, he learned.

This man's friend saw his growing ability and also wanted to learn to carve wood. The friend signed an apprenticeship agreement. The first day he sanded—just sanded. The next day wasn't much better. Even though the work he was asked to do was the same as the first man's, he grew bored, broke his apprenticeship contract, and stopped coming.

Years went by. The first man became a master carpenter, well known far beyond his town. The second man never developed the skill to make more than a rickety stool.

Was it unfair that the first became a master, and the second did not?

This life is like an apprenticeship. We decide here, do we really want to learn to be like God? We will not get very far in this life. All our attempts are but a toddler's stumbling steps compared to God's work and His goodness. But if we keep learning at His feet, I believe in the eternities we'll grow to become what we can't even imagine now.

The Carpenter

Gentle hands with strength
carefully carve thin layers,
revealing the soul of the wood.

Strong hands with gentleness
bend, but not break, the pieces,
fitting them into perfect form.

The violin sings from
what once was boards.
The wood becomes music
through the carpenter's hands.

Gentle hands with strength
carve thin layers from my soul.
Selfishness, pride, annoyance
fall in shavings, leaving a lightened heart.

Strong hands with gentleness
bend, but not break, my life,
forming me with trials and joys,
shaping me as far as I will follow.

And some day when
I see Him face to face,
I'll weep with joy for the
Carpenter Who formed me.

INGREDIENT: REPENTANCE

"Repentance is God's ever-accessible gift that allows and enables us to go from failure to failure without any loss of enthusiasm. Repentance isn't His backup plan in the event we might fail. Repentance is His plan, knowing that we will."
—Lynn G. Robbins[1]

Signs of Repentance

Pecan, who was having a rough day, made some *kick-me* signs and stuck them on his siblings' backs. His consequence—make kind notes to stick on the backs of people. After some thinking and brainstorming with me, he wrote for each of his siblings, "Hug him" or "Hug her", and "Psst, don't tell anyone I'm here".

Cherry joined in the fun and wrote the following:

- On Pecan: Applaud this guy. He's awesome!
- On Apple: This girl is simply lovable!
- On Lime (because Lime was trying to be scary): Runnnn! This guy is scary. Runnn! (Lime loved it.)
- On Huckleberry: You want this guy on your team!
- On Strawberry: She's so cute!

- On me: Hey! This girl's a Mom Superhero!

We can support and cheer each other in the repentance process.

Family life is full of learning, growing, apologizing, and trying again. In many ways this is what repentance is. A chance to change and opportunity to become closer to God. The Swedish word for repentance literally means "to turn around." I'm so grateful for daily opportunities to turn around.

Physician

> He healed the sick,
> caused the blind to see,
> the lame to walk
> the issue of blood dried up.
>
> The people marveled
> at the outward healing.
>
> But it was the
> inward healing,
> the softened heart,
> the opened mind,
> the soul expanded,
> that was the
> greater miracle.
>
> The physician is not
> here to heal the whole
> but those ill.
>
> And we are all sick

in our own
unique way.
We all need
His healing touch.

—Inspired by Mosiah 16:8-15

~

Repentance happens best in a place of safety, a place where we can make mistakes and learn from them without fear.

One way we try to make a safe place for mistakes and change is how we correct a child. This is our usual correction process:

- Obtain calm
- "Please tell me what happened."
- "What can we do differently in the future?"
- "Let's practice."

A little explanation of each step.

Obtain Calm

No effective teaching happens while angry. Yet it is so easy to slip into yelling, criticizing and jumping to conclusions, if I don't take time to calm down first. And my children don't hear much if they aren't also calm.

I learned from another mother to say, "I know you want to tell me something, and I want to listen, but we both need to be calm before we talk."[2] This validates that they want to tell me something and that I will listen, but also ensures that the conversation happens where we can actually hear each other.

This is when a time-out is helpful (even for me), but I have to make sure we come back to discussion after we are all calm.

. . .

Example: The Meltdown

One time my seven-year-old wanted to watch a specific movie, got a "no" answer, and fell into a screaming, kicking fit. I tried to reason with him but it made the meltdown even worse, and I realized I needed to give him space to calm down before we could talk at all.

While he tantrumed, I prayed for understanding for the deeper reason behind his actions.

After some time he came to me mostly calm (though sniffling with tears) and after a big hug, we read some picture books together. Only after all that did we talk about what happened. He told me that he prayed and asked Heavenly Father's help. I'm grateful for God's blessing to both of us in staying and obtaining calm. I needed His help, because it is hard to remain calm in the face of a meltdown.

Please Tell Me What Happened

This gives clarity to the situation. I want to hear what happened from all involved. Sometimes I assume something happened, then find out my assumptions are completely wrong. This question also gives them time to see more clearly what happened. Sometimes they are unaware that they did anything wrong. Sometimes they are very aware of it, but don't know how to verbalize it or are ashamed.

It is important to focus on the action without condemning the person who acted. "This is what went wrong" instead of labeling "you are—"

What Can We Do Differently in the Future?

Often this step is a brainstorm session. "What are options that you could do in this situation?" For example if a child got frustrated with a younger sibling's noise and shoved them out of the room, we could think of three things that they could do instead. This helps them find freedom and power in choosing instead of just being told what to do.

This is also a place to apologize to whoever was hurt. "I'm sorry for... It was wrong because... next time I'll... what can I do to make it up to you?" (More on this later.)

Let's Practice

A direction heard is quickly forgotten. A direction acted on stays longer. An action repeated starts to become a habit.

Practicing is the hardest part for me to remember to do. It takes time. But when I'm willing to take the time to practice with them and praise them in the process, we have less repeated negative behavior and more of the positive new actions. Over the years, new behaviors have become reflexive. We have a long way to go, and plenty of backtracking, but it is encouraging.

Often there is no time to practice right in the moment. I use the whiteboard or my notebook to remind me that this is something we need to practice. Other times I'm tired and don't have the presence of mind to deal with it. I'm grateful to tag-team corrections with my husband. We help each other when we are at our wits' end.

The above is a daily process in our family. And so is individual repentance. It is a daily turning to God for help in seeing what went wrong, what I can do to make it right, and what I can change in myself with God's help; and practicing making those changes.

Apology

It is easy to say "I'm sorry" and not change. The following steps help us think about what we've done and take actions to change. I often laugh (silently) at the responses to these questions.

"I'm sorry for..." The kids come up with some interesting things, and it helps me see what they are seeing. For example: "I'm sorry for playing with you. I didn't know you were grouchy." This was after a brother teased his little brother. So we talked about the difference between joking around with someone and laughing at someone.

"It was wrong because..." Again this gets some interesting comments. We try to focus on how it impacted others. "It was wrong because: it hurt your feelings, was thoughtless, and so on."

"Next time I'll..." I love this step as the child gets to find something to do instead. "Next time I'll ask if you want to play something with me and we can decide on something together."

"What can I do to make it up to you?" This gives both people a place to reconcile. Often the request is a hug or just "give me space" (depending on if the child is extroverted or introverted).

These are the same steps that Jesse and I take when we apologize to our children.

∾

Other Thoughts on Repentance

Slow is Fast and Fast is Slow

My husband taught me that *with people, slow is fast and fast is slow.* Meaning that when I try to rush a person in changing, then their change is slow, but when I take the time to slowly work with them, the change happens faster (and is longer lasting).

Practice and Prayer

In a Family Council we discussed adding prayer and practice to any correction. We called it "prayer and practice opportunities." It involves a positive and learning focus instead of a correction focus. Cherry called it PPO, then, being silly, she said, "everyone in favor of PPO say, 'Pink Piglets and Oranges.'"

Perspective

It is best to judge our actions against the commandments and not someone else's actions. The commandments give a solid standard. If we judge based on others' actions, we can always find someone who is doing better or worse than we are, and we can either justify our own actions or feel depressed at how poorly we are doing. Our Savior takes us from where we are and helps us move toward Him.

Focus

As a parent, I have daily opportunities to intercede or to let things go. If I nitpick at little things then I hurt the relationships and lose the opportunity to influence on the big things. I rate importance based on God's commandments, safety, and how it impacts relationships. It is important to know the difference between a sin (against God's commandments), a mistake (not studying for a math test), and a preference (wearing mismatching clothes).

I also try to let natural consequences for actions happen as much as possible, so that I can support my kids in learning instead of handing out punishments.

My goal is not to have perfect children, but to teach my children so they can grow into responsible adults who know how to follow God, are open to making mistakes, and who evaluate and improve their lives.

Careful

In what I see,
do I look to praise
and improve?

Be careful.

When teaching another to improve,
temper the criticism with
honest praise.
May the positive words
lift the person high above the
weighting negative emotions

lest they esteem me an
enemy.

For my heart closes,
my ears dull,
when met with
constant
criticism.

Mote and Beam

And why beholdest thou the mote that is in thy brother's eye, but considerest not the beam that is in thine own eye?

Or how wilt thou say to thy brother, Let me pull out the mote out of thine eye; and, behold, a beam is in thine own eye?

Thou hypocrite, first cast out the beam out of thine own eye; and then shalt thou see clearly to cast out the mote out of thy brother's eye.

—Matthew 7:3-5

In parenting, often my "beam" is impatience or frustration. And when I'm trying to correct (remove a mote from a child's eye) while feeling these emotions, I cannot help the child. But when I've asked for Heavenly Father's help and calmed down (removed the beam from my own eye), then I'm able to help my child.

A Family Discussion: A Parable on Repentance

Some people look at sin and say, "I can always repent." This is like saying, "I can always heal," and jumping off the roof of a house.

If I were to jump off the roof, break my neck, and become quadriplegic, I'd have severely limited my options. I could wish all I want to take the action back, but I'd still be living with the consequences.

What if I found out I could regain full mobility—but only if I went through strenuous rehabilitation? I could choose to do all I could to heal even though it was hard. Or I could choose to not make that struggle, and live with very limited mobility.

Our Savior can be compared to a physical therapist who goes through intense work each session to help someone else heal spiritually. Our Savior worked harder and suffered more for each of our individual sins than we ever will feel as we go through the work in the healing process (repentance).

That doesn't mean that we don't have any pains or suffering as we heal (just like physical therapy). But the other choice of not putting in the work, not changing our lifestyle, not progressing, will mean we are stuck with something that will continue to deteriorate, and if we eventually choose to repent, the process will be that much harder, though our Savior will still be there to help us.

So if we ever find ourselves justifying breaking a commandment—something that God has given us for our joy and protection—remember the cost.

Note: I used severe physical disability as a parable for repentance, but physical disability is not a sin in any way. I truly admire the strength and resilience of those who do live day to day with lifelong challenges.

Blessings of Repentance

At family Scripture study we talked about the Savior's atonement and our repentance. We compared the cleansing of the atonement and repentance to the ability to heal. I said, "Imagine you couldn't heal. That every scratch you got would stay with you through your whole life." Then Pecan made an even more vivid comparison. "What if every mosquito bite continued to itch and bother you?" We all cringed and shivered. It is an apt comparison. Without the atonement and the ability to repent, even if we never committed any huge sin, every little sin would continue to itch and annoy us through eternity.

Advocate

He felt my struggles,
He suffered my pains.
He knows each of my
weakness and faults—
He paid for them
with His blood.

And knowing my
imperfections perfectly,
He pleads my cause.
He pleads that I may enter heaven,
broken as I am.

He pleads, "Father,
behold the sufferings and
death of him who did no sin,
in whom Thou wast well pleased.

"Spare these My brethren
that believe on My Name,
that they may come unto Me
and have everlasting life."

He advocates for me
with understanding,
justice, and mercy.

May I turn to Him,
my true hope
in eternal judgment.

—Inspired by Doctrine and Covenants 45:3–5

Rebellion, Repentance, and Choice
Mosiah 27:8-37

One of the sons of Alma... became a very wicked and an idolatrous man. And he was a man of many words, and did speak much flattery to the people; therefore he led many of the people to do after the manner of his iniquities. —Mosiah 27:8

The father, Alma, prayed for his wayward son, that he might "be brought to the knowledge of the truth" (Mosiah 27:14). This is a powerful lesson. He didn't pray that his son would repent, though I'm sure it was the deepest desire of his heart. Instead, he may have realized that truth allows us to choose.

As a parent, I sometimes want to compel a child to change, but I've learned from this story that I need to teach them actions and consequences so they can make choices, patiently love and nurture them, and pray that they may come to the truth. A compelled change is only superficial and temporary. I want my children to develop strong moral muscles in choosing as well as wise reasoning.

Mortal Struggles

We each have mortal weaknesses—things we struggle with. For some it is temper, for others it is being bossy. As parents, our job is to recognize those weaknesses in our children, and love them as we help them develop tools to specifically address those weaknesses. The weakness doesn't excuse them from obeying God's commandments; it just means it takes more work and more loving support to obey the commandments in that area.

We pray and consistently work with children in their specific struggles, but we also try to keep the balance that this is only part of our interactions with that child. If it becomes the majority of the time, then we know that the deeper issue is our relationship and that needs to be nurtured before learning can happen. Some children may always struggle with their specific weaknesses. I know I still struggle with being a good listener. But we hope that they will get better at recognizing when they are struggling, pause, implement tools for that struggle, and then move forward on a different path than the one on which they were going.

Teaching involves listening with the intent to understand them, brainstorming together, and practicing. We do lots of practicing, so hopefully new habits become stronger than old tendencies.

Simon and Humility

Acts 8:9, 13, 18, 20, 24

When Simon heard the gospel, he changed his life and his occupation. But he still had much to learn. He—like all of us—made mistakes and misunderstood many things. When he offered money for the power to bestow the Holy Spirit on people, he was rebuked. Instead of getting defensive, he accepted the rebuke and asked Peter to pray for him. He humbly kept on the path of following Christ.

Repentance and our Savior

"Although the Savior has power to mend what we cannot fix, He commands us to do all we can to make restitution as part of our repentance. Our sins and mistakes displace not only our relationship with God but also our relationships with others. Sometimes our efforts to heal and restore may be as simple as an apology, but other times restitution may require years of humble effort. Yet, for many of our sins and mistakes, we simply are not able to fully heal those we have hurt. The magnificent, peace-giving promise of the Book of Mormon and the restored gospel is that the Savior will mend all that we have broken. And He will also mend us if we turn to Him in faith and repent of the harm we have caused. He offers both of these gifts because He loves all of us with perfect love and because He is committed to ensuring a righteous judgment that honors both justice and mercy."

—James R. Rasband[3]

The Worth of a Soul

Trembling under Ammon's sword
the king of the vast
Lamanite nation
swore an oath.

"If thou wilt spare me
I will grant unto thee
whatsoever thou wilt ask,
even to half of the kingdom."

Half his kingdom
for his life.

Through Aaron's teachings,
the king's perspective expanded.
He promised:

"I will give up all that
I possess, yea, I will
forsake my kingdom, that I may
receive this great joy."

All his kingdom,
for eternal life.

Then he learned,
it isn't his kingdom

God wants, but him.

He bowed himself
upon the earth and
raised his voice to heaven.

"I will give away
all my sins to know thee,
and that I may be
raised from the dead, and be
saved at the last day."

All his sins,
to know God.

This is the
greatest sacrifice,
and the path to
greatest joy.

—Quoted portions from Alma 20:23; 22:15, 18

INGREDIENT: FORGIVENESS

God of the Broken

The blind, begging by the wayside.
The leper, unclean and shunned.
The woman taken in adultery.
The social pariah publican.
All rejected.

Except by Him.
He hears the blind man's pleas.
He touches the leper's decaying flesh.
He lifts the woman to a new life.
He enters the publican's home.

He loves each one.
Seeking and ministering,
One by one.

And one by one
the broken find

peace and healing.

—Inspired by 2 Nephi 26:27-28

I'm grateful for my husband and the level of trust we've grown to over the years. He's forgiven me for times when I've been at my lowest; when I've complained, criticized and been hyper-sensitive. I've done the same for him. Forgiveness gives us a space to learn, do better, move forward, and grow closer together instead of being stuck in what happened in the past.

I want my children to know that I love them no matter what they do. I want them to feel safe to tell me anything. And I want to show them examples of forgiving others who have hurt me. Most of all I want them to turn to God and seek the joy of His forgiveness and the peace of His help in forgiving others.

~

Forgiving others

So that contrariwise ye ought rather to forgive him, and comfort him, lest perhaps such a one should be swallowed up with overmuch sorrow.
—2 Cor 2:7

In our family, we have daily opportunities to forgive. A brother teases, a sister gets frustrated, a father yells, a mother criticizes. Emotions hurt. Words sting. And it is hard to let go. But forgiveness is as important for the person hurting as for the person who hurt. The peace of forgiving someone is as sweet as the peace of receiving forgiveness. Both bring joy, a lightness, and an unburdening.

Forgiving doesn't mean ignoring what happened. We ask our children to come to us when hurt physically or emotionally. If it is by a sibling, then we work with that child in the repentance process. If it is by someone else, then we talk with that person and work to figure out what is going on. And if it is by someone who is dangerous in any way, we set up healthy boundaries.

Favorite Quotes on Forgiving Others

"The Savior offers you ... the ability to *forgive*. Through His infinite Atonement, you can forgive those who have hurt you and who may never accept responsibility for their cruelty to you.

"It is usually easy to forgive one who sincerely and humbly seeks your forgiveness. But the Savior will grant you the ability to forgive anyone who has mistreated you in any way. Then their hurtful acts can no longer canker your soul."

—Russell M. Nelson[1]

"'I, the Lord, will forgive whom I will forgive, but of you it is required to forgive all men' [Doctrine and Covenants 64:10]. It is, however, important for some of you living in real anguish to note what He did not say. He did not say, 'You are not allowed to feel true pain or real sorrow from the shattering experiences you have had at the hand of another.' Nor did He say, 'In order to forgive fully, you have to reenter a toxic relationship or return to an abusive, destructive circumstance.'"

—Jeffrey R. Holland[2]

Blotting

Part I
The blood seeps red into the carpet,
a nosebleed caught too late.
I scowl as I scrub at it.
It smears and sinks deeper.

I scrub harder.

If I try long enough and hard enough,
it will come out.

The next day, the stain is back,
larger and only a little fainter.

How do I get rid of it?
I need help.

I learn about blotting.
I saturate the stain with hydrogen peroxide,
then take a clean, white cloth,
and gently dab the stain, pulling out the moisture.
Little by little, the blotting pulls out the stain.

Part II
The hurt feelings seep into my heart.
A misunderstanding caught too late.
I scowl as I scrub at it,
my heart filled with complaints.
It smears into my other emotions and sinks deeper.

I scrub harder.
If I try long enough and hard enough,
I won't feel this anymore.

The next day, the hurt is back,
larger and only a little fainter.

How do I get rid of it?
I need help.

I turn to my Savior.
He saturates my life with his grace.
And with His pure and perfect love,

He gently pulls out the hurt and the pain.

It takes time.
I have to keep coming to Him.
And in the end,
I can love my neighbor again.

~

Forgiving Ourselves

> Nevertheless, notwithstanding the great goodness of the Lord, in
> showing me his great and marvelous works, my heart exclaimeth: O
> wretched man that I am! Yea, my heart sorroweth because of my flesh;
> my soul grieveth because of mine iniquities.
> —2 Nephi 4:17

I sometimes struggle with scrupulosity. "To have scrupulosity, as opposed to simply being scrupulous, is to desperately seek an unattainable state of righteousness. It is to feel immense guilt at every minuscule failure."[3]

During this struggle, and through God's grace, I've learned some very important lessons about forgiving self.

1. I don't pay for my sins. My Savior does. He suffered and paid for every one of my flaws, faults, sins, and mistakes. All He asks me to do is to repent and turn to Him with my burdens. My faith isn't in my ability. It is in Christ!

2. Though the Scriptures say when we repent God remembers our sins no more, it never says that we won't remember them. Instead, it says we won't remember the *pain* of our sins. "I could remember my pains no more; yea, I was harrowed up by the memory of my sins no more"

(Alma 36:19). Alma still remembered his sins. He recounted them to his sons and used his experience to help them. I believe we are blessed to remember our sins and faults so we can learn from them. It's the pain that is taken away. I've felt the sweet peace of forgiveness and love. Often. Repeatedly, as I've sought it.

However, in times of scrupulosity it is like pulling a scab from a healing wound or cutting off a scar, because the remembered sin becomes equivalent in my mind to an unrepented sin. I reopen the wound, causing the pain to come back and creating an even larger scar as a result. It isn't that I haven't repented, but rather that in my mental struggles, I re-injured myself.

3. The Scriptures say, "there cannot any unclean thing enter into the kingdom of God" (1 Ne 15:34). My scrupulosity causes me to worry that I missed some little sins and didn't repent of them and that will keep me from exaltation. Yet this again is putting faith in my own ability instead of faith in my Savior. He doesn't ask me to be perfect now. He asks me to trust Him, to love Him, to grow and change through Him. He paid for everything, even the things I've missed. I don't reach heaven by meticulously catching and "paying for" every little mistake—but by following my Savior and being changed through Him. Scrupulosity puts the focus firmly on me. Faith puts the focus firmly on my Savior.

4. Scrupulosity and shame are forms of prejudice. We pre-judge and condemn ourselves when God openly offers repentance, change, and becoming whole. C.S. Lewis said, "I think that if God forgives us we must forgive ourselves. Otherwise it is almost like setting up ourselves as a higher tribunal than Him."[4]

5. In seeking relief, it's important to remember what repentance is and is not.

Repentance Is:

- Recognizing a wrong.
- Confessing and apologizing for it to the involved parties.
- Reconciling and trying to make right with those hurt.
- Resolving to do better and seek God's help in changing.
- Recognizing current imperfections and that the struggle with the same issues will likely continue, and not giving up.

Repentance is Not:

- Pulling the scab from healing emotional wounds and repented-of sins.

6. Years ago, I read an article on the Shame Cycle. I saw myself in that and wanted a healthy alternative. As a family, we created the Faith Cycle (see next section). I use this tool when I feel myself pulled into the dark storms of scrupulosity.

7. Scrupulosity is real. I can't just make it go away, any more than someone with depression can make that cloud go away. Rationally, I know the thoughts and emotions related to scrupulosity are false, but when in the midst of it, it is emotionally and mentally overwhelming. I'm grateful that I only have bouts of it and don't have to deal with it constantly.

8. I may always have struggles with scrupulosity. It is one of my refining trials in mortality. I love the Scriptures. They cut through the lies of Satan and help me see through the irrational emotions of scrupulosity. I'm grateful for parents who've always loved me and treated me as a beloved daughter to them and of God. I'm so grateful for the peace and grace of God. And for His healing power. I know He loves me. I know He wants me to return to Him. I know that as I keep

following the path He set, in my imperfect stumbling, that I'll make it because of Him.

A family discussion: Shame vs. Faith Cycle

As mentioned above, we read an article[5] that shows the Shame Cycle and how destructive it is. We talked about this article as a family and wondered what would be the healthy cycle in contrast to the Shame Cycle. This is what we came up with:

Faith in Christ Cycle
This leads us to trust God and grow through our mistakes.

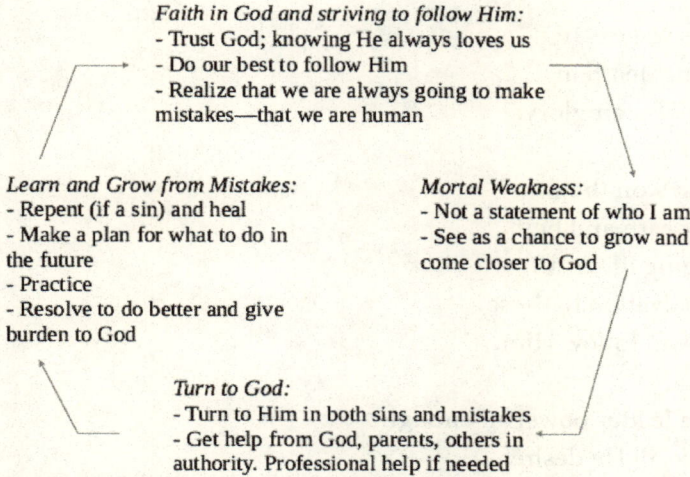

Faith in God and striving to follow Him:
- Trust God; knowing He always loves us
- Do our best to follow Him
- Realize that we are always going to make mistakes—that we are human

Learn and Grow from Mistakes:
- Repent (if a sin) and heal
- Make a plan for what to do in the future
- Practice
- Resolve to do better and give burden to God

Mortal Weakness:
- Not a statement of who I am
- See as a chance to grow and come closer to God

Turn to God:
- Turn to Him in both sins and mistakes
- Get help from God, parents, others in authority. Professional help if needed

Shame Cycle
One of Satan's tactics to stop us from progressing.

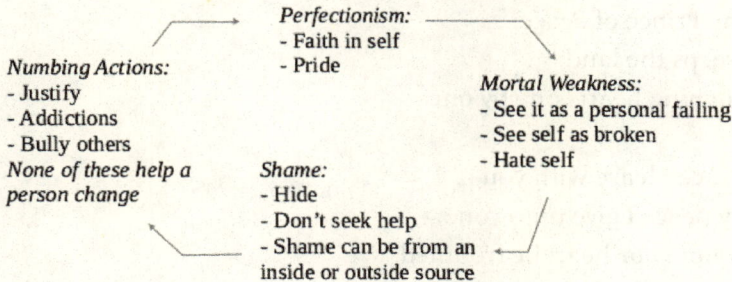

Perfectionism:
- Faith in self
- Pride

Numbing Actions:
- Justify
- Addictions
- Bully others
None of these help a person change

Mortal Weakness:
- See it as a personal failing
- See self as broken
- Hate self

Shame:
- Hide
- Don't seek help
- Shame can be from an inside or outside source

When we put our trust in Christ, and turn to Him in our weaknesses, we will grow and improve—even if it seems halting and snail slow. Repentance isn't a place of shame, but rather a way to heal so we aren't stuck in shame or numbness. I'm so grateful for the miracle and joy of daily repentance. I need my Savior each day. He is my peace and my salvation.

~

Prince of Peace

Kings wage war
trailing death in
wake of their glory.

Christ won the war
over death and hell.
Bringing life to all
and salvation to those
who will follow Him.

He's a leader powerful enough
to take all He desires.
Instead gives His life
to give us the choice of joy.

The Prince of Peace
sweeps the land,
touching hearts one by one.

"Peace I leave with you,
My peace I give unto you...
let not your heart be troubled,
neither let it be afraid."

No matter what happens,
in Him I find rest and hope.
In Him is Peace.

—Inspired by John 14:27, Isaiah 9:6, 2 Nephi 19:6

Metamorphosis

Metamorphosis I

Fleshy caterpillar
whose view is the
next leaf to eat
was never meant to
stay earthbound.

Her parents brightened the sky,
flashing color of soulful joy.

Yet the change seems
too drastic, too hard.
Why give up the known life,
a full stomach, a shaded shelter?

Her parentage pulls.
She imprisons herself
in silk threads,
giving up what once was,
trusting in changes to come.

It hurts!
Everything shifts.
The old self melts away
and the new is unfamiliar.

She pushes from her threads,
spreads her wings,
and enters her destined skies.

Metamorphosis II

Fleshy human
whose view is the
next comfort
was never meant to
stay earthbound.

Her parents brighten the universe
with unbounded creations,
Filling every inch with love.

Yet the change seems
too distant, too great.
Why give up the known life,
the contentment and comfort?

Her divine parentage pulls.
She binds herself with
covenant cords,
giving up what once was,
trusting in promises to come.

It hurts!
Everything shifts.
The old self melts under
soul-refining trials.

She trusts in Christ,
holding fast to Him,
finding peace.

He carries her,
granting a perfect
brightness of hope.

Her heart expands,

spreading wings of charity,
and takes flight.
—Inspired by 2 Nephi 31

We don't have to fit a certain mold to be acceptable to our Savior; we just have to be humble enough to turn to Him and follow Him. He cares about who we are and who we are willing to become, not so much who we were.

INGREDIENT: RESPECT

...he inviteth them all to come unto him and partake of his goodness; and he denieth none that come unto him, black and white, bond and free, male and female; and he remembereth the heathen; and all are alike unto God, both Jew and Gentile.

 —2 Ne 26:33

One day Cherry came to me with a bemused look. "Mrs Jones (name changed) told me that I make her son uncomfortable because I don't shave my legs."

"Well," I said, "do you want to shave your legs? It isn't necessary for health or hygiene like showering. Many people like it, but it's really up to you. Do you like it?"

"I don't."

And we left it at that. It wasn't a moral or health issue, just a fashion decision.

We want Cherry to be comfortable as she is. If she dyes her hair, shaves her legs, or pierces her ears, to do it because she wants to, not because a neighbor, a family member, or society tells her she should.

We also want to be considerate to Mrs Jones, seek to understand her point of view, and be kind even if we don't agree.

It all comes down to respect. Respect for self and respect for others.

This world is full of people and we each have our own unique way of seeing things. We each are multi-faceted. We must see people from many sides to truly know them. Yet, seeing someone from many sides takes work. It is often easier to pre-judge them based on superficial first impressions or labels. In fact, the word "prejudice" comes from "pre" and "judge". When we are prejudiced, we pre-judge someone without really knowing them or seeing them as a person.

To get past this pre-judging and truly know a person, we need to extend respect. Respect them enough to assume that they may be (and usually are) so much more than we perceive. Respect them enough to take the time to get to know them. And if we don't have that time, respect them enough to withhold judgment.

When we take the time and effort to extend respect, we move away from pre-judging, past tolerance, and we come to care about the person —no matter who they are.

Note: God is the opposite of prejudice. He knows us perfectly, but He withholds judgment until after we've lived a full life of choices. He respects us and our freedom to choose. And He stands ready to help us as we turn to Him.

Rough Edges

This is for my friends who see the world vastly differently than I do, and who create so much good with their unique strengths and talents.

The Lord gave us
clashing personalities.

I crash against you,
alternating between feeling
I should be more like you
and wishing you could be
a little more like me;

then it wouldn't be so hard
to be around each other.

But neither is a good solution.
We aren't meant to be alike.
We have different talents,
different strengths and weaknesses.

So I turn to my Savior to help me see
the good in you without losing who I am.
He opens my eyes and my heart
to try again, to move forward, to forgive.

And as we learn to work together,
bringing our strengths,
developing patience with our differences,
and supporting each other in our weaknesses'
we begin to rub off each other's rough edges
and see outside our own narrow view.

Through time and our Savior's help
we are polished.
You shine more brilliant a ruby;
I glow more clear a sapphire.
Unique friends.

Note from Danny Smith, a brother-in-law: Rubies and sapphires are both "corundum (aluminum oxide). The differences lie in the mineral inclusions (our unique expertise and talents), but the primary mineral is the same (we are all children of our Heavenly Father)."

Personalities

My husband and I have six children with six different personalities.

Some are high energy, with boundless noise. Others are reserved. Some have a quirky sense of humor. Some have a short fuse. We each have different things that bother us. We each have different interests. Mathematically, in our family we have fifty-six overlapping, interconnected relationships (8 people interacting with each other, 8x7). Misunderstandings and conflicts happen.

We try to respect our differences and give space for those differences, instead expecting everyone to be the same. Our home is a good training ground for learning to work with a variety of people.

One way we can respect differences is allowing people freedom to do a task in their own way. I like to pile all the dishes in the sink and soak them before washing them. Some of my kids set all the dishes to the side and take one dish at a time to wash in the sink. Neither way is the "right" way. The same can be said for any number of tasks.

Keep Names Safe

Part of respecting others is not gossiping. If something needs to be addressed, then we try to respect a person by talking to them (or the proper authorities). We can keep each other's names safe in our conversations.

I love the example set by a young man in our neighborhood. When he heard gossip, he told the people to stop it, then he found the person being gossiped about and took time to be their friend.

Respecting Self

Pecan got corrected for something, and he fell apart, telling me that he was horrible and could do nothing right. I heard the correction and it was calm—so this was a symptom of a deeper problem. I prayed to know how to help him and had the impression to have him read through copies of letters I'd written to grandparents, and find thirty accounts of good things about him. He made a tick-mark on a paper every time he found one. His whole attitude changed. I'm so grateful for family stories to help us see beyond our emotionally narrowed view of ourselves.

Respect and Confidence

When we respect others, we can let go of the need to compare ourselves to them and try to be better, or fear we are worse, than they are. Instead of a contest, we can build confidence in our own talents while admiring others and cheering them on.

Withholding Judgment

We need to know the different types of judgement. We need to make judgements for safety and truth. But we are never to condemn others. That is left to God and the justice system.

In our family, we try to speak with respect as we discuss hot topics at the dinner table: politics, wars, protests, gender identity, vaccines, etc. We don't know all the facts, so we try to understand with the facts we have right now, and be open to learning more, all the while standing in the defense of freedom, the innocents, the marginalized, and the vulnerable.

It is sometimes hard to not get emotionally invested, especially when someone has hurt us personally. It takes consistent prayer to withhold condemning judgment, and to act purely on safety judgments (like "I need to only see this person in a public gathering.").

My favorite talk on withholding judgment and acting in peace is "Love Your Enemies".[1]

Given Much

Because I have been
given much,
I, too, must give.

Loaf of bread and
glowing fire.
Simple daily needs.

But also patience,
compassion, and
withheld judgment
for those who see
differently than I.

Can I give a
soft answer and
benefit of the doubt
to those who lack kindness?

Can I love
those who are
hard to love?

For some days,
I lack kindness and
am hard to love,
yet my Lord
loves me still.

Because I've been
given much,
I, too, must give.

- Inspired by the hymn "Because I have Been Given Much"

Disagreeing without being Disagreeable

I believe many things to be true and important, and these beliefs and values are not always the same as what the people around me believe. I can show respect to those I disagree with by:

1. Listening to their side and asking clarifying questions. I have to be careful not to make any judgmental statements but just seek to understand. I know I've reached at least a partial understanding when I can summarize what they've been telling me and they say, "That's it," or "That's right."[2] (This doesn't mean I agree, just that I understand.)
2. Then stating my beliefs. I need to be calm, clear, and unapologetic, and not push them to agree.
3. Finally finding common ground between our beliefs. There is usually something.

We may both go away from the discussion firm in our own beliefs, but we will also have a better understanding of each other.

Two Evolutions of Disagreeing

One family scripture study centered around the problem of contention. Pecan stated an evolution of a disagreement:

Disagreement > Contention > Anger > Fighting > Feuds > Wars

However, disagreements are not wrong in themselves. We learn from each other as we have different points of view. If we all agreed on everything, we'd stagnate. So we have to learn how to go in a positive direction with disagreements:

Disagree > Obtain Calm > Listen > Come to Understand > Extend Kindness/Respect

At no point is it necessary to agree. We can understand each other, at least each other's emotions, and extend kindness and respect.

Ignoring or avoiding disagreement stops this process of understanding and often goes into the contention path. However, if we've come to an understanding of each other (or at least I've come to an understanding of the other person even if they don't seek to understand me), then it is fine to just agree to disagree and drop the subject.

. . .

Disagreeing and Safety

I've found occasionally that a person I'm disagreeing with doesn't want to agree to disagree, even after we've gone through the steps above. For example, one person said, "No, I will not agree to disagree. You will not cancel me!"

Usually that refusal is combined with toxic communications such as mocking or backhanded implications that I'm morally, intellectually or spiritually inferior for having a different opinion.

I'm still trying to figure out what to do in such cases, especially when the person is someone that I come in frequent contact with. So far I'm doing the following:

- I don't bring up the controversial topic.
- When they bring it up, I ask if we can talk about something else and if they don't, then I leave the room (or chat group) if possible.
- I set up safety boundaries on where and how often I associate with such people.

Note, this is what I do after I've taken time to understand their perspective and they've said I've understood it correctly.

Labels

Labels and categories are helpful when trying to organize things like spices or books. I like to put all my history books in one place and all my novels in another. Categories allow me to quickly find the book I need and judge a new book against the ones I've already read.

However, labels and categories can be damaging when applied to people, because they narrowly define—putting them into neat little boxes of ethnicity, gender, religion, locality, employment, interests, or even what clothes they wear.

If I hear that a person is (fill in the blank) and judge them only based on what I've experienced with others in that category, I am limiting my ability to really know them.

I strive to teach my children to live the gospel, love their family, develop their talents, and not worry about the labels that others give them. I also hope they will learn to actively look past the labels placed on others and seek to get to know them as individuals.

INGREDIENT: LOVE

A new commandment I give unto you, That ye love one another; as I have loved you, that ye also love one another. By this shall all men know that ye are my disciples, if ye have love one to another.

—John 13:34-35

The Savior suffered and died for us, not because we deserved it, but because He loves us and Heavenly Father. I can serve and sacrifice for others, not because they deserve it, but because I love them and I love Heavenly Father and my Savior.

Who is our neighbor? The parable of the Good Samaritan answers that vividly. All people, from those in our own homes to those in distant lands, are our neighbors, especially those we come in contact with. How do we treat those closest to us as well as those who irritate us the most? We are to love our enemies, those who persecute us, those who drive us nuts, and those who want nothing to do with us.

How Do We Love Our Neighbor?

I've already talked about forgiveness and respect. I'll talk about service in the next chapter. Here I'll talk about seeing the good in others, and about time, consistency, boundaries, listening, gentleness, and patience.

~

See the Good in Others

> Let us not therefore judge one another any more: but judge this rather, that no man put a stumbling block or an occasion to fall in his brother's way.
> —Romans 14:13

Everyone has good in them. And almost everyone wants to be noticed. We can show love by noticing and sincerely complimenting others. Others' words of kindness to me have often changed an overwhelming day to one where I'm bouncing with happiness, even though what I faced hasn't changed.

Even a simple "thank you" can change someone's day. A specific "thank you" goes even further.

When we are struggling in a relationship, one of the balms is finding something to praise or thank the other person for. Just as gratitude brings complaints into perspective, thanks and compliments bring criticism into perspective.

For example, I try to teach using the sandwich method: by sandwiching the teaching between compliments. It is more palatable and better received, plus it helps me see the good in the person and be more loving in my teaching.

Grandma Stewart

"My talent is to
appreciate others' talents."

She sees good in everyone.

You can't be around her and not feel
better about yourself and life.

She sends a birthday letter to
each child, grandchild, and great-grandchild.
Not just a card,
but a handwritten letter,
telling in specific ways how wonderful
that person is, and how much
she loves them.

She's my role model
of a joyful saint.

Compliment Game

One day, two of my sons had several conflicts. In a moment of desperation came a needed inspiration. We played the compliment game.

They took turns saying something that they liked, admired, or saw good in their brother. At first it was really hard for them to think of anything. So I gave some suggestions and said, "You can just repeat what I say for the first few times." After this priming they came up with their own. They changed from anger to a begrudging, "I guess he's good at that," to, "Wow, my brother is pretty cool!"

I'm so grateful for Heavenly Father's guidance in helping my sons see the good in each other.

Weeks later, they chose to play the game on a walk.

Compliment Tag

Competitive and equally paced,
brothers tag each other along our walk.

The tags grow to vigorous slaps on backs,
back and forth, till I command, "Stop. Just jog."

They jog along, glancing at each other.
The older tags the younger, but before I can speak,
he says, "You're great with puzzles."
The younger tags back, "You're awesome with Legos."

Back and forth they tag each other,
filling the air with their compliments.

∼

Time

"In family relationships love is really spelled t-i-m-e, time."
—Dieter F. Uchtdorf[1]

We have the same 24 hours each day. They speed by quickly. I don't think we need to fit more into each day, but use the time we already have together to really be together.

Meal Time

Meal time is a wonderful connection point. We talk about our days —both the good and the bad. We muse over geeky topics (like how magenta isn't really a color on the light spectrum, but a combination of two) then delve into serious topics. This is lightened by dad jokes. When Jesse and Pecan get going, they'll continue the puns until we are all groaning. Dinner conversations are interspersed with asking for more food, urging our youngest to eat, and trying to hear each other over enthusiastic noise. It's delightful chaos. And sometimes not so delightful. But it is a daily part of life, and a time that is essential for growing in love for each other.

. . .

Daddy/Kid Outings

When we had four kids, we started doing Daddy/Kid Outings. Each week, one of them got an evening with Daddy, just the two of them, where the child chose the activity: marble mazes, video games, Legos, puppet pretends, frisbee, and pillow fights. Over the years, the night of the week has changed and we added two more children to the mix; and still the kids look forward to their turn at this weekly evening for a month and a half.

Mommy/Kid Time

My strengths are different from Jesse's. I sometimes play games, but my time with kids usually involves reading to them and learning together. The wonderful thing is, the kids love both the play time with Daddy and the quieter time with me. We don't have to do the same sorts of things.

Work Time

Dishes, canning, weeding the garden, and other work are all time in which we can talk as a family and enjoy being around each other. (See more in *Ingredient: Work*.)

Suffer the Little Children

The multitude crowded to hear His words.
They bombarded Him with questions.
Many tried to trip Him in His teachings.
He must have been weary.

Then mothers came with their little ones,
begging His blessings on their children.
His disciples, seeking to spare their master,
rebuked them and sent them away.

But Jesus called after:
"Suffer little children to
come unto Me."

He blessed them.
He loved them.

He asks us to receive them,
to love them,
to learn from them,
to become like them.

Little children,
"Submissive, meek, humble,
patient, full of love."

"For of such is the kingdom of God."

So when I am weary,
my day overflowing with "must dos",
and my children need me,
begging in actions
grumpy, upset, or rude,

may I remember to
set aside the multitude of tasks
clamoring for my attention
and gather my children.
Bless them, love them.
Give them my time,
my attention, my prayers.
For of such is the kingdom of God.

—Inspired by Luke 18:15-17, Mosiah 3:19

≈

Consistency

Consistency in our rules and how we act toward our children leads to a feeling of safety. And that safety provides a place where love can grow.

One day Jesse asked, "What is a rule you like in our home?" Some of their answers were:

Apple: "Be nice and gentle."

Cherry: "Clean up what we get out."

Huckleberry: "Two hours of play-outside time before media on any day. I like the media more and we are nicer to each other." (We've learned this through trial and error, and it certainly helps our high-energy children.)

If we didn't have consistent rules, it would be like the Game of Mao[2] where we'd constantly be guessing at what we should be doing and stressed about what the consequences are. Specifics would be discovered through trial and error.

We've also learned that it is important to have the same rules for everyone in our family, including adults. If our children are expected to be gentle, be honest, not yell, etc, then we should also follow those rules. Bedtime is one of the few exceptions—it is based on age, so our teens get a later bedtime than our younger children (though there are many nights I'd love to go to bed at the same time as the little kids).

≈

Boundaries

"Our job as parents is to set clear boundaries and lovingly hold to them. And our children's job is to test those boundaries."[3] Some days, some of my kids really do their "job," and I really have to work at the "lovingly holding to boundaries" part.

"Lovingly holding to boundaries" means empathizing with the other person's emotions, being calm and listening, but still holding firm to the boundaries set. Let the boundary be the consequence and not an emotional outburst. It goes back to making sure everyone is calm before trying to address an issue.

It also means we need to be careful not to set too many boundaries. If there are too many rules for a child to remember or explain, then there are too many rules. We try to keep them simple and clear.

We also set boundaries based on specific needs in our family. Many of our kids are mildly on the autism spectrum. Things that are perfectly fine for those not on the spectrum can cause emotional havoc in our family. Little things like food coloring, lots of media, changing plans without warning, or too many people often lead to full-out meltdowns. By identifying triggers, we are able to set up boundaries so the triggers happen less often and so we can practice what to do in those specific situations. Before we get into a situation where we'll likely encounter a trigger, we do "just-in-time instruction" to help us practice and mentally prepare.

All these boundaries start with counseling together as parents then discussing it as a family. The results are a combined effort (see the *Family Council* chapter).

∼

Listening

Along with being noticed, being heard is a vital love language in our family. Huckleberry especially thrives on this. He will stop playing and come tell me all about the pretend he is doing. He'll leave in the middle of a video game that he's watching Daddy play with his older siblings, to tell me the storyline. I'm still learning to stop what I'm doing and listen.

Jesse is really good at listening without judgment, just listening until a person (child or adult) is done talking. Then he waits in silence, processing what was said, and giving the person time to also just be, before speaking. It is one of his talents.

We try to listen even if the topic doesn't interest us (though often the interest grows as we listen). I have no interest in playing video games, but my husband and kids love to tell me about them, and we geek out together over cool video game ideas. They listen when I share reader reviews for my books and celebrate with me.

Child interviews give us time to listen to our children tell about their fears, their struggles, their interests, and the cool thing they saw that day. These child interviews are a time to first listen, and then, if the child wants it, help find solutions. Sometimes the child just wants to be heard and figures out their own solution in talking.

~

Gentleness

Gentleness in word, emotion, and touch invites a feeling of love, while roughness in these areas quickly drives wedges between people in our family.

Gentleness in Touch

We have some children who thrive on physical touch. They are constantly hugging, tackling, wrestling, poking, tickling, etc. Some of it is gentle, some of it is playful roughness, and some of it is hurtful. We are still trying to help them find the balance in this.

For gentleness in play, we tell our kids that wrestling and other rough play happens outside. The rough ground actually encourages them to be a little more gentle in their wildness. We also practice stopping right away when someone says "stop" or is acting as though they don't like it.

For gentleness when angry, we have a rule that if someone is angry, frustrated, or otherwise feeling negative, that they back away from other people or fold their arms so they don't hurt someone. This simple rule has been an essential starting point for being able to think instead of react.

We try to hug the children who thrive on touch often. Foot rubs, back rubs, and holding them close while watching a movie also help them feel loved. We've also learned to give more space to those children who only want occasional hugs.

. . .

Gentleness in Word

> A soft word turns away wrath.
> —Proverbs 15:1

Though this seems old fashioned, the simple words *please, thank you,* and *I'm sorry* are powerful. When I ask a child, "Will you please take out the trash?" or "Please keep to inside voices," they respond much better than if I demand, or worse, yell it. "Thank you for setting the table," or "thank you for helping make dinner," leads to more helpfulness.

Gentleness in word means no mocking. A painful comment followed by, "I was only joking" cuts like a knife. Sarcasm isn't funny to the recipient of the barb. Gentle words build others up, help them see the good in themselves and others, and are understanding. Gentle words are often preceded by listening.

Gentleness in correction leads to honesty and openness. One day my seven-year-old took out the trash and accidentally tipped over the large garbage can. His older brother went out to help him right the garbage can and saw that it had scratched the car. Instead of hiding the fact, they told us about the scratched car. Jesse and I thanked them for their honesty, then talked about what we could do in the future to avoid tipping over the garbage cans. We decided to put the garbage cans in a different part of the driveway. I'm so grateful that we were gentle in our words.

Gentleness in Emotion

Someone can be *gentle in action* in that they are never physically rough, and *gentle in word* in that they always use polite language, but still be cold, uncaring, or manipulative to others. Gentleness in emotion is being aware of others' emotions and being there for them. It means giving people space. It is not taking advantage of or manipulating others.

Gentleness Practice

Jesse and I were counseling together about how the boys defaulted to pretending to fight whenever they were pretending. It's a standard boy thing—and not bad—but it would be nice if they expanded their horizons. We came up with a plan that after dinner every day I'd do dishes, and the kids would have a choice of either helping with dishes or go to a "Pretending Class" with Daddy. He directed them in various "pretends" that didn't involve violence: exploring, creating, helping others. (We've done this practice for a few weeks at a time over the years, as needed.)

～

Patience

"Success is going from failure to failure without loss of enthusiasm."
—Winston Churchill

Life is a learn-on-the-go journey. It is full of *try, fail, evaluate, revise, and try again*. We need patience with each other and with ourselves. To me, patience is moving forward in what we can do, trusting God in what we don't yet understand, and allowing for mistake after mistake after mistake. Each time, getting up, evaluating, and trying again with the new knowledge gained. Patience is also giving others this same space and time.

Planted Seeds

The rich young man came running.
"What shall I do that I may inherit eternal life?"

Then Jesus, beholding him, loved him,
and asked him to give up all and follow.

Can I behold others,
seeing their goodness
and their potential?
And beholding them,
can I love them,
seeking the gift of charity?

My job isn't to change another.
Instead, I'm to
see others,
love them,
invite,
and allow
them to choose,
while always loving

and so plant seeds
that someday may grow.

—Inspired by Mark 10:17-21

INGREDIENT: COMPASSION

And behold, I tell you these things that ye may learn wisdom; that ye
may learn that when ye are in the service of your fellow beings ye are
only in the service of your God.

   —Mosiah 2:17

Many Decembers ago, we started decorating our Christmas tree with
paper angels. When a child did an act of service, they wrote it on an
angel (or told me so I could write it) and we put it on the tree. It helped
change the focus from "What am I going to get this Christmas?" to
"Whom can I serve?"

A different year, I set aside a day of the week (Mon—Sat) for each
child to have one-on-one time with me. We served someone and then
we did something fun together. Both activities were often simple, and
we tried to keep the total time from 30 minutes to one hour. (I'm hoping
to do this again this summer).

The wonderful thing is that sometimes the child found the service
more fun than the planned fun activity. I asked one daughter what she
wanted to do for fun after we had visited an elderly neighbor, and she
said, "Wasn't that the fun? I love going to see her!"

There are so many ways to serve. It doesn't have to be big. Giving a listening ear, a hug, or a helping hand are all service. Reading to a child, cheering their rickety block tower construction, giving focused attention, playing Go Fish are also service. Service can take money, but most often it takes time.

Sabbath Service

Our Savior served every day, even on Sunday. Since Sunday is a day of rest from our usual jobs and schooling, we try to serve in some way. It can be a phone call or letter. One daughter likes to type in the info from old records for family history. Others will read to younger siblings. It helps us look beyond ourselves and remember to love God and our neighbor.

Birthday Cards

Cherry is always drawing. One year she asked for the birthdates of all her grandparents, aunts, uncles, and cousins. Then she put together a calendar with the birthdays. It hangs on our fridge. She and her siblings trade off drawing a birthday card for each family member as their birthday month arrives. They usually do this on Sunday as a Sabbath service.

Masks

In 2020 we made hundreds of masks (cloth and medical) to send to different humanitarian projects. We listened to music and told jokes as we cut, pressed, sewed, and sewed, and sewed. Even our youngest helped stack cut fabric for the next step. At the end of that crazy year, when we each shared a highlight of the year, one child said, "It was so much fun to make masks."

Friendship Seeds

After a major fight between two brothers, we discussed friendship seeds. Their friendship is like a hard seed. But as they water and give it light, the seed will sprout and it can grow into an amazing friendship. Both brothers want this, so we came up with some light and water to give their seeds.

Light:

- Pray morning and night for help in being a better friend.
- Pray for help to understand the other person.

Water:

- If angry, stop and listen (or get away from them until calm).
- Ask the other person what they want to do. And take turns deciding what to do.
- Spend time building something together—like legos or blocks. They want to build a treehouse this summer, so they are working on smaller projects now so they can communicate better with each other.

After we talked, Huckleberry said, "When I get home from school, I'm going to water my friendship seed."

This is a current learning experience, as of writing this book. I'm adding my prayers to theirs. I feel hopeful that as we continually check back on how this experiment is going, Heavenly Father will give us further insight on what to do.

INGREDIENT: WORK

Apple loved to dress up. At age three she changed clothes ten or more times a day. The laundry piled up. After talking with Jesse, we decided the kids were old enough to learn how to fold clothes and put them away, even her.

The first laundry day, I gathered Cherry, Pecan, and Apple around piles of washed clothes. They helped sort them into piles of their own clothes. Cherry and Pecan had a smaller pile of clothes, and after some simple examples, they filled their baskets with folded clothes, put them away, and went to play. Apple stared at her pile and started to cry. I knelt next to her and helped her fold or hang each of her clothes. By the end she started to do it herself. And when Daddy got home from work, she proudly showed him what she'd done.

And as a result Apple stopped changing quite as often, and with the kids' help folding, laundry no longer felt so daunting.

Family life—rather, life in general—is full of work. From employment to laundry, it permeates each day. Work is often mundane, involving the same actions over and over again. And this is a blessing because it allows for conversation and growing relationships as two or more work side by side. It also brings a feeling of accomplishment.

Following are some lessons we've learned through work over the years.

Chore Charts

When our oldest was four, we made chore charts with pictures for our two older kids, then made one for Jesse and me so they could see us marking off our chores.

Cherry saw a blank spot on my chore chart. "Mommy, you need to draw a picture."

"Should I draw you and Pecan, for taking care of you?"

"No, draw Mommy and Daddy."

I created a spot on my chart for Mommy and Daddy time. I liked this because it showed our children that taking time for each other is important.

Cherry's Chart

Our four-year-old
draws a grid with
scribbles and dots.

"This is my chore chart."
She points to the scribbles.
"Get dressed,
Make bed,
Wash dishes,
Plant garden,
Help mix cookies.

"And this is my fun chart:
Play in the park,

Read Scriptures,
Read books,
Paint,
Sing songs,
Pray,
Give hugs,
Dance,
Chinese jump rope."

She points to the bottom of the page.
"Rules!
Ask Mommy,
Obey,
Be nice."

Delegate

Sometimes the choice is not between *to do* or *not to do*, but *to delegate*. Over the years I've learned to delegate: to let a child take responsibility for a task, give them basic instruction, allow them space to act, praise them for their efforts, and be patient with their growth. In this process, they've grown in capacity and confidence.

Saturday Chores and the Vacuum Monster

We divided up the bathroom and vacuuming chores between the kids. With everyone helping, those weekly chores all got done in an hour each Saturday. Then we had free time to do family fun. The kids were excited to help with the chores, so we taught them the basics then let them try.

Pecan ran downstairs, turned on the vacuum and started yelling—a long, loud, droning yell. We ran down after him and asked what was wrong. He explained that he didn't like the noise of the vacuum so he yelled to cover it. After the surprise of his statement had time to sink in, and we stopped laughing, we got the construction ear protectors from the garage. Pecan wore them when he vacuumed and no longer yelled.

We learned that resistance to a chore isn't necessarily because children don't want to do it, but because of some other stimulus. Many years later, Pecan, as a teen, was vacuuming and yelling. He couldn't find the ear protectors and had resorted to his old coping mechanism.

Teaching to Do Dishes—and in Turn Gratitude

Lime had become entitled in his words and actions. He complained about any little task I asked him to do, and he demanded things instead of asking. While praying about what to do, I had the thought, "teach him to do dishes". So he and Huckleberry started doing lunch dishes with me. It was amazing how this one thing impacted us. A few days after starting this, Lime asked to help with breakfast dishes. He started asking—instead of demanding—more often, and he helped more willingly and was more grateful.

Some things I relearned in this process: When teaching a child a new skill, make sure to set aside the time for it. Slow is fast and fast is slow. If I take the time to help them learn something well and not under stress, they get it firmly and can move forward with it. This is obvious for things like potty training. But it is also true for things like chores, educational skills, and life skills.

Stewardships

After child number six entered our family, we created our *Stewardship Board*. It focused on three main areas of daily responsibility: chef buddy, work buddy, and child helper. When we first started the stewardships, it was just our three oldest kids who took part, but then the younger ones joined. The stewardships rotate each week. This, along with Saturday chores, covers most of the basic skills our children will need when they grow up and start their own homes.

Chef Buddy: This child plans the menu for the week, helps me put together a shopping list for what they planned, and helps make the dinner each night. Now we have two children who help with this each evening.

Work Buddy: This child helps me in whatever project I'm doing (or at least in one of the project). They range from yard work to laundry, reconciling bank accounts to mending. I sometimes tailor the projects to the child when I'm planning the week. Though I try to rotate through the skills so they each learn them.

Child Care Helper: This child helps younger siblings with getting dressed, reads to them, or even changes a diaper. This one has phased out as our youngest grew to where she didn't need (or want) help. I guess my youngest kids will have to learn child care with nieces and nephews.

Each of the stewardships is a *work-with-Mommy* type job. We work side by side, talking, learning, and sometimes laughing together. My kids tell me about their dreams or some cool idea.

Stewardships are more difficult to do consistently during the school year, and we adjust as needed. Sometimes the chef buddies only help with a couple meals in the week if they are swamped with homework. Sometimes I save work buddy jobs for Saturday. Flexibility is vital.

No Nagging

My parents taught me, "Tell a child once, then take their hand and do it with them."

Nagging only leads to frustration and a child learning to ignore. When I remember to stop what I'm doing and help them get going, the child learns to respond right away, and emotions are more level on both sides.

With teens, it is a bit different. I still try to get their attention, and if they continue to ignore, tell them what privilege they lost for a short time (usually the thing that distracted them from obeying).

No Gender-Specific Chores

We want our sons and our daughters to be competent in cooking, cleaning, yard care, child care, and finances. One area we haven't taught them is auto care (like changing the oil), because neither Jesse nor I learned that. There are no gender-specific chores, and they rotate through them all. Certain children definitely are better at certain chores, but that's because of their individual interests and talents and not their genders.

Disagreeing Appropriately

We taught our children to disagree appropriately. Basically that means when they don't like an instruction, they need to calmly say, "May I disagree appropriately?"[1] then explain a 'why' they don't want to do it and give an alternative. Most often their reason is "Can I do something else instead?" or "May I finish what I'm doing first?"

One day I asked Pecan to put the food away. He said, "May I disagree appropriately ... may I ... can I ... can I ... Oh, I don't want to disagree, I want to put the food away."

Another time Huckleberry came in and asked if he could use the hammer to break up the ice on the cement. I told him no. He asked to disagree and explained how he'd be very careful. Jesse and I discussed it, gave him some instruction on carefulness, and decided to let him do it.

Initiative and Resilience

I hope my children will grow to be resilient, and interestingly enough, patience combined with encouragement leads to resilience. As we praise them for their effort, acknowledge that *yes it is hard*, and encourage them to keep trying, they grow to do hard things.

We also want them to take initiative. Again encouragement, praise, and reasonable expectations lead to this. Our children have surprised us with many things they started and completed without our help.

For example, one time Pecan (then ten years old) looked through our scrap wood and found the lower half of a stool—we'd cut off the top to use as a step stool in the bathroom—so the bottom was just the four legs with four cross pieces. He also found a small square of plywood and nailed it to the legs, making a seat, then duct taped over the seat covering the splintery wood. I didn't even know he was making anything until he'd finished. The stool is sturdy and still in use many years later.

On the other hand, we've learned to be careful in correction when initiative ends up in a mess. Apple found a broken jar of jam in the garage and vacuumed up the pieces. We never were able to clean the jam out from the interior of the vacuum, and it grew mold. We ended up buying a new vacuum. The cost of the new vacuum was worth Apple's initiative. We made sure to repeatedly praise her for making that effort, even as we taught her how to handle a broken jam jar. She's continued to take initiative since then—sewing many fun dolls and stuffed animals without patterns.

Note: We do have rules about power tools. The kids don't use those without our permission and supervision.

Note on reasonable expectations: Nitpicky criticism cripples creativity.

Poor Spot of Ground

> And it came to pass that the servant said unto his master: How comest thou hither to plant this tree, or this branch of the tree? For behold, it was the poorest spot in all the land of thy vineyard.
>
> And the Lord of the vineyard said unto him: Counsel me not; I knew that it was a poor spot of ground; wherefore, I said unto thee, I have nourished it this long time, and thou beholdest that it hath brought forth much fruit.
>
> —Jacob 5:21-22

Often the poor ground with nourishing touch is the best growing situation. I strive to let my children have challenges and struggles, all the while nourishing them, providing a loving atmosphere in which they can find peace in the midst of their struggles.

~

Family Projects

Yard

When we bought our house, it came with three-quarters of an acre of land. Over the years we've tended gardens, raised chickens, fought spiny Russian-olive suckers and mended sprinklers. Unlike the weekly inside chores, the yard has often involved big projects like putting in several hugelkultur or building a chicken run, interspersed with seasonally changing tasks.

Though some of the big projects lasted for only a year or two (we currently don't have chickens), we grew as a family as we planned, worked, laughed, cried, tried again, and revised our plans. Our *failures* in our yard are more memorable than our successes, and have given us much experience.

The Broken Water Line

One day we came home to find a geyser in our lawn. Our sprinklers are on canal water, the house is 50 years old, and the sprinkler system is perhaps as old, with many use-what-you-have patch jobs. One of those patch jobs failed under the vibrations of road construction.

Jesse was at work, so the kids helped me turn off the water main, then we dug until we found the broken pipe. We ran to the hardware store in our mud-splattered clothes, bought parts, and returned to make repairs. The repair didn't hold. We tried using other parts. A new section broke. Frustration exploded into laughter as water squirted into faces. Jesse came home to a family of mud monsters and a dinner time of stories.

The difference between a good disaster and a bad disaster is often who we share it with. Many a time of intense frustration has turned into laughter because someone could see the humor in the situation. We also discovered that some things take repeated effort, learning a little more each time. It took all summer until we finally got the water line fully repaired. It was a brown-grass summer.

Homemade Christmas

Each year at Christmas at least some of the gifts are homemade. Apple sews stuffed animals. Cherry molds figurines or makes paper dolls. Pecan once made a wooden sword and shield. We've worked together to make a box hockey game[2] and a wooden cube puzzle[3] with a drawing from each of us on the six different sides. The finished products have the sweet irregularities of many different hands, at varying levels of expertise, working together. We aren't attempting perfection, but we allow each person to give of themselves without criticism.

On Christmas Day, everyone is more excited to give their gifts than to open their own. The anticipation, the joy in creating and the joy in giving, is why making Christmas gifts is one of my favorite family projects.

Canning Applesauce

I grew up canning applesauce with my family. Now every year or two we gather with my parents and local siblings to can a thousand-plus pounds of apples. This two-day marathon is full of hard work but also wonderful memories. It is a place of gentle teaching, passing on traditions, laughter, learning new ways of doing things, family togetherness, and encouragement.

Half Ton of Apples—A Harvest Haiku

Half ton of apples,
jumbled red, piled yellow.
Trailer sags sweetness.

Splash, giggle, splash more.

Small hands fill water barrel.
Apples rinse, shiver.

K'shnack, apple halved.
snik, snik, stem and blossom gone.
Tat-tat-tat, pieces.

Babe, on Mama's back,
leans to see what Mama's done
since a child herself.

Knives flash midst stories.
Chopping beats time to tales.
Poetry piles high.

Great-grandma, smile-creased,
long years not slowing quick hands.
We race to keep up.

Deep cookers bubbling.
Apples soften, white turns gold,
steam rich with orchard.

Papa and Daddy
heft cookers and toss dad jokes.
We dodge and chuckle.

Scoop, schlop, funnel full.
Apples separate, seeds—sauce,
glopping, spitting, hot.

Empty jars recall
last year's bounty—come again,
creamy, golden, sweet.

Grandma, hands fruit-stained,
guides child, love woven with skill.
Fill, wipe, cap, tighten.

Quarts bathe in boiling,
shoulders snug, hot bubbles rise.
Tickle air out, seal.

Jars, row follows row,
parade, boasting their treasures.
Harvest promise kept.

INGREDIENT: EDUCATION

Over the years, we've used several modes of education: homeschool, co-ops, and public school. Each has been wonderful in different ways. Here are some tools and ideas we've used along that path.

Code of Learning
1. *Learn in all areas of life (Doctrine and Covenants 88:77-80)*
2. *Evaluate the learning compared with truth.*
— *Use the gospel as a measuring stick*
— *Sift the empty from the wholesome*
— *Pray to discern truth from error*
3. *Apply the important parts to life (13th Article of Faith)*

Learn in All Areas of Life: There is no skill that only men or only women are good at. That dichotomy is a logical fallacy, perpetuated for far too long. There are certain skills that specific children are better at, but I want them to also become competent in the tasks they don't particularly care to do. To help learn in all areas of life, we have both formal learning in school and informal learning in dinner-time discussions, reading together, watching educational videos, and experimenting. Our discussions cover Shakespeare and space exploration, color theory and music history, logical fallacies and political platforms. We also learn in the practical areas of life: building, sewing, etc.

Evaluate Learning Compared with Truth: We use the gospel as a measuring stick. There is so much that the Scriptures don't talk about, but what they do talk about gives us a place to measure—especially in the social sciences. We also see what our church leaders say in official addresses (avoiding obscure references taken out of context). We compare against other data. We fact check, looking for reputable peer-reviewed resources (we don't do this every time, but we do it when there are arguments on both sides of an issue).[1]

There is so much information in the world. Only some of it is true and even less of it is important. It would be easy to fritter away a lifetime just looking at info. We try to sift through what we are learning and focus on that which has substance.

As we learn, we turn to God in prayer for help to discern between truth and error. There was a time Jesse and I took some classes on achieving goals. They had lots of good material, but some of it felt off. The more we got more into them, the more *off* the classes felt. We studied, prayed, and decided to stop taking the classes. The errors were too ingrained.

Apply the Important Parts to Life: Learning takes on meaning when applied. We read many books as a family, and we discuss how we can learn from the characters, both the good and the bad. We write on the whiteboard specific things we want to apply in our family, then practice them over a period of time.

∽

Try Again

Learning is full of mistakes. If we never failed, then we never really learned. I love what my dad's English professor taught: "This is not a writing class. It is a rewriting class. You are allowed to rewrite and resubmit your assignments until you are satisfied with your grade." From this, I've told my children, "If writers are allowed to edit, then you are allowed to do a problem or assignment again." As they work through the process of doing it again (and again as needed), they improve.

~

Logic

We were learning about formal and informal logic as a family. Here are some of the things the kids came up with. We were laughing as we came up with these.

Valid Arguments (but Not Sound)

Only brains are in your head.
Eyes are in your head.
Therefore eyes are brains.

Only hair is on your head.
Ears are on your head.
Therefore ears are hair.

On the other hand, with informal logic, we studied emotional fallacies.

- Be wary of any artificially raised emotions. Do not make any decisions while in this state.
- "If you need an answer now, the answer is no. If you give me

time—away from this emotion and at least a day, but up to a week—then the answer may change."[2]

- If you find yourself around someone who is artificially raising the emotions, get out—even if you paid money to be there.
- Note people that you find yourself getting into trouble with. They may be well-meaning people, but if they work off your emotions and you find yourself making unwise decisions around them, be extra cautious in making decisions when they are involved.

~

Family Discussions

Following are some of our favorite family discussions (these mostly happened at meal times). See also "Family Councils" for more of these.

A Thought on Necessities and Gratitude

One morning at breakfast we talked about what we couldn't live without. The kids—quite practically—said things like air, food, water... We added family and the gospel. Then we asked, "After those things, is there anything that we *couldn't live without*?" We decided no, but here are few things that would be very difficult not to have: the ability to create and freedom to go outside.

Heroes

We asked our kids, "Who are some of your heroes, and how are they a hero?" We got a huge, long list. The cool thing was the common characteristics:

- Helped others
- Kind

- Sacrificed
- Endured/didn't give up
- Influenced others to change to be better
- Accepted those different than themselves
- Saw people as people
- Often eccentric—didn't let what others thought about them influence them away from their path (some truly didn't care what others thought, while other heroes just put it in proper perspective.)
- Some of the heroes were strong or powerful. But that wasn't what made them a hero.

Hero Spotlight: Sam Gamgee, Parents, and our Savior

One of the most poignant moments in Lord of the Rings is when Sam tells Frodo that "I can't carry the ring, but I can carry you." As a parent, I've experienced that on both ends. There are many trials that I cannot carry for my children, but I can walk beside them and at times carry them as they carry their burdens. On the other end, I've felt my Savior's love as He's allowed me to carry my burdens so I can grow, but He's kept beside me the whole time and often carried me. In those times, I've still felt the burden, but I've no longer felt crushed by it.

∼

Odyssey of the Mind

One year the kids participated in Odyssey of the Mind[3]. It is "a creative problem-solving program involving students from kinder-garten through college." We loved discussing the creative conversation-starters at dinner. (Lists of these types of questions are on the Odyssey of the Mind website under "spontaneous problems".) Here are some of our favorites:

. . .

If you could go back in time and take a picture of anything, what would it be?

- The looks on the fish's faces when the Red Sea parted. The codfish is still stunned.
- The cloud of helium balloons that lifted the City of Enoch.
- King Nebuchadnezzar water-sliding down the hanging gardens.

Names things that grow bigger or smaller:

- Pride grows bigger before the fall.
- Family grows bigger with marriage.
- Water grows smaller when it melts.

If you could call anyone and ask any question, who and what would it be? For added fun; have someone else on the team answer the question.

- Hello, Mr. Potato Head. Don't you think it's about time to try a new vegetable?
- Hello, Mary Poppins. How does it feel to be practically perfect in every way? (Pecan answered: Stressful!)
- Hello, Mr. Einstein. How long does it take you to do your hair in the morning?
- Hello, T-Rex. How are you even talking on a phone with your short arms? (Answer: With a selfie stick.)

Name something lost or something found.

- Lost tooth

- Lost in thought
- Found your true self
- Then Huckleberry (age 4) said, "When we die, we lose our body and go up to heaven. Then later we get resurrected."

∾

Children and Youth Program

The *Children and Youth Program* focuses on "Following the Savior in all areas of your life"[4]. It helps children and youth make goals and improve their lives in four areas: spiritual, social, physical, and intellectual. We love how this helps our family keep balanced between the many different parts of life and draw closer to our Savior.

∾

Favorite Reads

My favorite way to teach is through reading good books to my children. We read together almost every day, and over the years we've found many treasures. Reading an example is often more powerful than talking about the desired action. These are our top family reads (outside of the Scriptures). It was hard to narrow it down to these. When I shared the list with the kids, they added several more of their favorites.

Nonfiction

- *The Hiding Place* by Corrie ten Boom
- *Little Britches* series by Ralph Moody
- *Passage to Freedom: The Sugihara Story* by National Geographic Learning
- *Shipwrecked at the Bottom of the World* by Jennifer Armstrong
- *Cheaper by the Dozen* by Frank B. Gilbreth and Ernestine Gilbreth Carey

- *Carry On Mr. Bowditch* by Jean Lee Latham

Fiction

- *Les Misérables* by Victor Hugo
- *A Single Shard* by Linda Sue Park
- *Maniac Magee* by Jerry Spinelli
- *Chronicles of Narnia* by CS Lewis
- *Ranger's Apprentice* series by John Flanagan
- *Book of a Thousand Days* by Shannon Hale
- *The War that Saved my Life* by Kimberly Bradley
- *The Evolution of Calpurnia Tate* by Jacqueline Kelly
- *Ella Enchanted* by Gail Carson Levine
- *The Queen's Thief* series by Megan Whalen Turner
- Lime said we had to include my *King Trials* and *Hearth and Bard* books, because they are his favorites.

Authors

- John Flanagan
- C.S. Lewis
- J.R.R. Tolkien
- Lloyd Alexander
- Jane Austen
- James Herriot

Poetry

- *Read-Aloud Rhymes for the Very Young* selected by Jack Prelutsky
- *Something Big Has Been Here* by Jack Prelutsky
- *One Hundred and One Famous Poems* compiled by Roy J. Cook

Picture Books/Short Stories

- *The Serpent Slayer: and Other Stories of Strong Women* by Katrin Tchana
- *The Ravenous Gown: And 14 More Tales about Real Beauty* by Steffani Raff
- *A Caravan from Hindustan: The Complete Birbal Tales from the Oral Traditions of India* by James Moseley
- *Mightier Than the Sword: World Folktales for Strong Boys* by Jane Yolen
- *The Gardener* by Sarah Stewart
- *Black and White* by David Macaulay (he also has amazing construction and science books)
- *The Monster at the End of This Book* by Jon Stone

Favorite Parenting Books (I didn't read these to the kids, but I've shared many ideas from them):

- *Boundaries with Kids* by Dr. Cloud and Dr. Townsend
- *A House United* by Nicholeen Peck

INGREDIENT: WHOLESOME RECREATION

All work and no play... you know the rest of the saying. Here are some of our favorite fun activities to do together as a family.

Active Fun

These are especially important for my children who need lots of movement in order to think.

Dancing: This is Cherry's favorite. She turns on music and dances every morning, no matter what else is happening. We sometimes play "Follow the Leader Dancing" where one person leads the dance for a song and everyone else tries to mimic their movements.

Racing: Huckleberry loves to race. He and I will race to the back of our ¾-acre yard and back until we are both too tired to run. I sometimes take the kids on the bike trail and we hike several miles, alternating between walking and running.

Climbing: Pecan is a good climber. He's climbed up our cherry tree and into the branches of our Russian olive. I've taught the kids to maintain three points of contact (two feet and one hand, or two hands and one foot) at all times. And so far they've been careful.

Jumping: Our trampoline is in use summer and winter. The kids shovel the snow off as needed.

Basement Jungle Gym: Several Christmases ago, Jesse and my dad installed small metal loops in the ceiling of our basement, each made to hold up to 200 pounds. We hung a climbing rope, a rope ladder, a swing, and monkey bars from the ceiling. When the weather is miserable, the kids climb all over downstairs. It is a sanity saver for our home.

Hiking: We love to go hiking. Moose, deer, hawks, eagles, ground squirrels, dragonflies, and a variety of wild flowers and plants have all filled us with wonder. I race the kids uphill and watch them race each other going down (I finally understand my dad saying that going uphill is easier than down). We sing hiking songs.

Johnny, Johnny Butcher Boy: "Split into two groups. Group 1 walks up to Group 2 and says: "Johnny, Johnny Butcher Boy, coming for a trade." Group 2 says: "What's your trade?" Group 1 says: "Sweet lemonade." Group 2 says: "Well, get to work and show us, if you're not afraid." The first group will then act out an activity: watering the lawn, changing a tire, playing baseball, etc. If the second group guesses the activity, they can run after members of the first group and try to capture them."[1]

We like to combine this with a water fight, where the chasers throw water balloons or wet sponges.

Other favorite active fun:

- Eagle Eye[2]
- Sledding
- Water fights
- Frisbee
- Bocce

$\approx$

Games that require Few or No Supplies

TELESTRATIONS

This is like playing "Telephone" with pictures.
Supplies for each person:

- stack of ten small papers, stapled at one corner
- pen

Game: To start the game, each person draws a picture—any simple picture—on the first page, then passes their stack of papers to the person on their right. Next, each person looks at the picture and on the second page writes a word or brief description of the picture. Then they pass it on. On the third page, the next person draws a picture based on the word or phrase. Alternate between word and picture each page without looking back at previous pictures or phrases.

As in the game Telephone, you end up with the idea changing as it gets passed around the circle. The best part of the game is looking through the pictures and words afterward and seeing how the meaning changed. It always results in lots of laughter! For example, how can a "tin can" become "Santa Claus" or "cute fluffy cat" become a "lightning-struck skunk"?

Even children who don't read or write yet can play. As long as someone else will read and write for them, the child can draw the pictures. We've even played this with our three-year-old.

PICTURE THIS (variation on Telestrations)

Cherry came up with this variation on Telestrations. Everyone had a dry erase pad (paper would work too). Then Cherry gave a simple description like "something tall and skinny" and then everyone drew and afterwards compared.

- "tall and skinny"—a giraffe and bare winter tree.
- "long ears and long tail"—long-eared and -tailed rabbit and a long-eared dragon.
- "small and pointy"—needle, hedgehog, rose with thorns, and pocket knife.
- "Something that has wings but doesn't fly"—castle (which has wings off the main building).
- "Flies but doesn't have wings"—flying carpet, wind, baseball in flight, and helicopter.
- "Jiggly and useful"—door stops, gel mouse pad, and blubber on a whale.

WHO, WHAT, WHERE

This simple game creates all sorts of silly scenarios. We play this whenever we are waiting—at the zoo, doctor's office, in line, etc. The only needed supply is an imagination.

One person thinks of a question and states the category of the question, but not the question itself. For example: I think, "Where does the pirate hide his treasure?" but all I say is, "I have a where." Everyone else thinks of a location. When everyone has a location, I state the question, and they give their pre-thought answer. This also works with "who" (a person), "what" (an item), and a "when" (time). We've sometimes included "how" (by doing an action) and "why" (the answer is in the form of "because...").

This gets us to think outside the box.

MAD LIBS

We love to do Mad Libs while washing dishes. One person will be the writer while everyone else gives words to fill in the story. We also do it with extended family, sending out the list of needed word types and then sending everyone the result.

You can buy a Mad Libs book or create your own stories. Apple likes to take short picture books and type up the story with blanks for many of the nouns, verbs, adjectives, and adverbs.

CRAZY CREATURES

Crazy Creatures is a drawing game where three people draw one creature, without knowing what the rest of the picture looks like.

Start by folding a paper in thirds, then marking over the folds the neck and hip marks (just two tiny dashes at each line). This allows the creature to line up. Draw the head of the creature, then turn over to the blank middle and hand to the next person. They draw the middle, then turn to the blank bottom and hand to the third person.

This game is great for all ages and drawing abilities. Even those who can only draw stick figures can add to the whimsy of the whole character.

SMURF

One person goes out of the room. Everyone else decides on a verb or action to be replaced with the word "smurf." The person who left the room returns to try and guess the word or action by asking individual people questions like "how often do you smurf," "why do you smurf," etc.[3]

CHARACTER OF MANY ARTISTS

Cherry, Pecan, and Apple created this game.

Supplies: Divide a paper into as many sections as there are people (either by folding or drawing lines). Each person needs one of these sectioned papers. We usually play with six people.

Game: Each person draws a character; a dragon, a fish, a scarecrow, or whatever they want. Then they pass their paper to the next person. Each person with their new paper draws the same character as was handed to them (so if they got a scarecrow from the previous person, they draw a scarecrow). But they draw it in their own style and with their own scene or modifications. They keep drawing and passing and drawing until everyone has drawn on each person's paper. In the end they have a character drawn in the style of many artists. Often the panels take on a story-like sequence of events. This game works with those who can only do stick figures as well as those who are fine artists. The combination of styles is what makes it so much fun.

Family Media Standard

Media can provide a wonderful form of family connection time, but it also can get out of hand. We created a family media standard to help keep it a positive activity.

Our standard addresses:

Where do we have screens in our home?

When does it happen?

How long? The only way we remember to keep to the time limits is a timer.

Content? We look to see if it invites or impedes the companionship of the Holy Ghost in our lives, and if it enlarges or restricts our capacity to live, love, and serve in meaningful ways.[4]

Media Violence

I've always loved action and adventure, as does my husband, which is probably why we keep coming back to this in our family media standards. We keep our movie ratings to PG-13 or less, yet there is such a range even within those ratings. We've had plenty of family discussions on the actions of different characters. Two of our sons are barometers on what lessons the movie or game taught. If it was of the numbing type of violence (which a majority of movies have at least in part) then they increase in unkind and rough actions. If it was of the non-numbing kind, then they usually don't.

What is media violence?
Here is our current definition:

Numbing violence: the hurting of another living being, human or otherwise:

- that is glorified or trivialized
- with little or no consequence shown

Violence that isn't necessarily numbing (but still could be): the hurting of another living being, human or otherwise that:

- shows consequences to the actions (to the one acting, the one receiving, and those around)
- is not glorified or trivialized
- is done to defend others or pursue justice without revenge, anger, or delight in the actions
- is done to serve as a cautionary tale (and shows the consequences)

Thoughts on Violence vs Natural Rambunctiousness
I want my children to delight in using their energy, in running, in racing each other, in active pretending, in wrestling and pillow fights.

This focus on striving to keep our media to non-numbing violence doesn't preclude those activities. Instead, I'm hoping it will help them be aware when they hurt someone accidentally so they stop and comfort the other person, and also that they will learn to control their tempers so they don't act in anger. Then they will develop compassion and emotional self control even as they play exuberantly.

INGREDIENT: FAMILY COUNCILS AND CHILDREN INTERVIEWS

Couple Council

Every Sunday Jesse and I council together. We start with prayer, seeking Heavenly Father's blessing and guidance as we council over our family. Then we briefly go over the calendar and projects. The meat of the council is when we talk about each child individually, discussing what they are doing well, where they are struggling, and how we can help them. We end it by discussing our marriage relationship and talk about anything that we could work to improve, and plan a date for the coming week.

This Couple Council prepares us for the Family Council. I write down topics to bring up in the Family Council. And if there are more than a couple topics, we decide what the two most important ones are to discuss that week and put the other ones in a list to address on a different week. We brainstorm solutions to specific issues but don't set those ideas into stone, because we will be talking about them with the kids in the Family Council and want their input.

Note: We try to keep our Couple Council to 30 minutes or less. Sometimes it is only 10 minutes.

∽

Family Council

Every Sunday (usually at dinner time) we hold a Family Council. This is a time to make decisions as a family. Our general format is as follows:

Opening the Council: Just for fun, we open the council by saying, "The Farb Family Council is now in session," or some derivative of that. Each week, we rotate who is leading the council, meaning they open it and introduce each section of it (exciting news, calendar, topics).

In one Family Council, Huckleberry was in charge. He had his mouth full of food, and so he couldn't start it understandably. Cherry said, "and translated: the purple hippopotamus is hungry." Huckleberry laughed and said, once he had swallowed, "the purple hippopotamus is hungry for exciting news. Who wants to feed the purple hippopotamus?" So we shared our exciting news and fed the purple hippopotamus.

Exciting News: We go around the table, and each person tells about something exciting from the previous week. It could be something they saw, something they did, something they are grateful for, etc. It is a time to celebrate each other's achievements and take delight in each other's interests.

Calendar: We go over what is happening the coming week, and double check with kids to make sure we have all their activities accounted for.

Topics: This is the main part of Family Council. The person leading the council asks if anyone has a topic. We always do serious topics first. Then we do fun or silly topics afterwards. The topics could be anything from rearranging chores, to practicing social skills, to what we want to do for an upcoming holiday. At the end of each topic we say, "All in favor, say 'aye'." Then, "All opposed, say 'nay'." We've had family members (including me) who have disagreed with the decision, which meant we returned to discussing the topic until we could find a solution that everyone agreed to (even if it wasn't exactly what they wanted). Sometimes the topic is set aside to be revisited the following week. Sometimes we do a trial run, to see how it worked, and then revise it the next week.

~

Examples of Serious Topics:

Many of the family discussions I've mentioned in the previous chapters happened as Family Council topics. Here are a few more:

Praying for each other: We keep a list of family and friends we are praying for. One day a daughter asked if we'd pray for her in her science class, and we realized we were missing out on praying as a family specifically for each other. The next Family Council, we asked each child for one thing we could pray for them about—something they were working on, struggling with, or seeking an answer to. Then we wrote these on the whiteboard. We update these as needs change, and we try to review them before we pray as a family. We even have a place for Jesse's and my prayer requests, because we also are very much in need of our Lord's blessings.

Media Standard: We once started watching an adventure-based cartoon as a family, and we were really enjoying it. But as the series progressed, certain elements appeared that went against our family media standard. After Jesse and I counseled with each other, we sat down in our Family Council and asked, "If this cartoon was made with real people wearing the same things, would you want to watch it?" The kids' reactions were immediate—with many loud "No!"s. We then discussed the pros and cons of the cartoon, and whether or not we should keep watching the cartoon. In the end, with some sad misgivings—because most of us wanted to see what would happen—we decided as a family to not watch it any more.

Examples of Fun Topics:

Terrarium Space Suit

We talked about a proposed moon settlement and asked the kids what they'd want if they were to live on the moon. Pecan said a space suit. And then someone said a space suit with a plant inside of it so it could change the carbon dioxide back to oxygen. It would be like having a terrarium helmet. Now I'd love for one of the kids to draw a comic with a terrarium helmet or backpack space suit. The biggest challenge would be to find a plant that changed out air fast enough.

The Sneeze

If you could have something happen when you sneezed, what would it be?

Cherry said, "When I sneezed I'd get better from any illness."

Jesse added, "It would cure everyone in the building."

Pecan said, "Go sneeze at the hospital and help everyone." Then added, "Travel wherever you want."

We all laughed as we pictured sneezing and then flying through the air backwards to a different state.

~

Child Interviews

Every Sunday (yes, our Sundays are full of counseling together), we sit down with a child to see how they are doing. We try to meet with two children each week, so they each get this one-on-one time every three weeks. We ask four questions and listen.

. . .

What is going well? This is a time to hear what our child is excited about, what they enjoy, and celebrate with the child.

What is difficult? I have to remember to not start brainstorming for solutions right away when we get to this part. It is important to just listen as they talk.

What can we help with? This is where, if a child wants help, they can specifically ask for it (though if they mentioned something that is difficult and they don't ask for help, I'll usually ask if we can help at this point of the interview). We talk about what is going on and offer ways we can support them. We brainstorm on what to do. For example, Huckleberry was having problems with bullies at recess. We practiced asking the bully to stop, and if he didn't, then talking to a teacher. We checked back with Huckleberry later on how the situation was going. And it did improve.

What else would you like to talk about? This is usually just a fun topic, and filled with lots of laughter or curious brainstorming.

BONUS INGREDIENT: ORGANIZING

Here are some of my favorite tools with which to bring a semblance of order to the always changing playing field of life.

Catch-All Notebook

I keep a notebook by my bed, one in my purse, and one in the kitchen. These are my catch-all notebooks. I "catch" any info I want to remember, usually in half sentences and partial thoughts. At the end of the day I sort the info into my journal, to-do lists, calendar, shopping list, etc. I label each entry in my catch-all notebook with a symbol so it is easier to sort.

Categories and Symbol (My symbols don't translate into a typed character. Use whatever symbol is easiest for you.)

Journal: J — About once a day I record the journal entries in a typed bullet journal. Sometimes I expand on a thought, but usually it is a bunch of disjointed snapshots of life. Most of this book came from those journal entries.

Calendar: C

Shopping: S — I also put "menu" under this symbol.
To-Do: T — I write these up on the whiteboard.
Writing idea: W

Here's an example of what a page may look like:

J: What did Helaman want his sons to remember? (Helaman 5:4-12)
 Keep the commandments of God
 Remember who named after
 Be humble (don't boast)
 ... (shortened for the example's sake)

T: Clean the gutters

S: Olive oil, soy sauce

J: Apple and Cherry decorating backpacks. Apple drew a sun on hers and Cherry is drawing dragons on her brothers' backpacks.

C: Dentist, Sept 8th, 10:30

T: Call Kezia

S: Parchment paper

J: Apple tried to pierce her own ears this morning using the tip of an earring. I asked if she'd like to get her ears pierced and she decided she doesn't. Laugh and sigh.

W: Research naginata

T: Practice times-tables with Lime

It looks crazy on the page, but it works for me. I'm sure there are many ways to modify it.

~

Daily Sheet

Each day I have some consistent activities as well as things that change based on the day. I use my "Daily" sheet to help me keep track and do what is most important first.

I print it, slip it into a page protector, and use wet erase markers to mark it. The wet erase stays until I use water (a damp paper towel) to wash it off so I don't accidentally rub something important off (plus dry erase markers stain the page protector). I reprint as things change: start of a school year, new goals I'm working on. But the sheet often stays for months at a time, helping me organize my day.

It has three sections: Daily, To Do, and Schedule.

Daily: These are the most important parts of a day, from personal Scripture reading, to reading with children, to exercising. I put a spot to check off the action when I'm done.

To Do: This section is blank. I write (with a wet erase marker) the tasks I'd like to accomplish that day. Sometimes they happen. Sometimes they get moved into the next day. I cross them off as I finish them.

Schedule: This section is also blank. I write the scheduled items for the day.

Here's a simplified version of it.

Daily's		To Do
5a __	Personal prayer, scripture study, journal	
6a __	Family Scriptures / get ready	
...		
7:20 __	Kids' school	
__	Exercise	Schedule
__	Serve	
__	Write	
...		
5:30 __	Goal reports / Family read	
...		

≈

Family Whiteboard

In our kitchen we have a 24"x36" whiteboard, salvaged from the dumpster at my husband's work. It has a few chips' and it took tons of vinegar to get all the stains off it. It is the central planning and discussion board for our family.

Example of the Family Whiteboard

Everything shown below is written in wet erase marker. And then I write in the changeable parts with dry erase (except on the Daily sheet, as explained above).

Menu				Daily		
Sun:						
Mon:						
Tues:						
Weds:						
Thurs:						
Fri:						
Sat:						
Weekly						
Sun	Mon	Tues	Weds	Thurs	Fri	Sat
To do		**Pray for**				
Family Use (this is about half of the white board)						

Whiteboard Explanation

Menu: We plan the menu each week and write it here, along with reminders (like "soak beans")

Daily: Explained in previous section.

Weekly: What is happening in the week. I write any repeat items (like daddy/kid date) in wet erase marker, so I can erase some items while keeping others.

To-Do: This is my running list of to-dos. None of them are assigned a specific date. I pull items from this list and put them on my daily sheet (under To Do). And if I don't get them done, I put them back onto this list. I have a longer list on my computer, but this limited space on the whiteboard, helps me focus on what is most important.

Pray for: Explained in *Ingredient: Prayer.*

Family Use: We don't actually label this. It is a horizontal line drawn across the middle of the whiteboard, and everything below that line is for family use. Kids draw on it. We use it in Family Council for brainstorming and planning. I teach math concepts. Pecan draws geeky visual jokes. It is a place for creativity.

～

Self Evaluation

I can't do everything. I don't even want to try. Yet as life goes on, many things get added to the busyness, and many things get out of balance. Every six months or so, I do a self evaluation on what is working, what needs to change, and how to go about making changes. It is a time of prayer, study, and pondering.

Sometimes I feel good about adding something new to my plate, and other times I feel strongly that it is time to simplify (often a combination of both). We are constantly adjusting as our family changes, as kids grow older, etc. What was right for our family last year isn't necessarily right for our family this year. There are some things that are always right (God's commandments, kindness...) but so much else is dependent on the situation.

BONUS INGREDIENT: PIANO CALLS AND OTHER SPECTRUM TOOLS

Since I've spent sixteen-plus years parenting and several of my kids are slightly on the autism spectrum, I've picked up a few tools. The following are some of my favorites.

Piano Calls – Attention-Getting Method

We developed the "piano calls" to help get a child's attention. It involves a short melody that is connected to a specific person or action. Because it is music, it connects to two sides of the brain and penetrates my children's super focus. We started by using them on the piano because it sounds throughout the house, but we also sing it if we are not around a piano.

Kinds of Calls:

- Everyone call: Lets everyone know to come right now.
- Five-minute warning: lets everyone know that they have five minutes before the *everyone call* will happen and to find a stopping point for whatever they are doing.

- Individual calls: specific to each person (even my husband
  and I have one). These range from the opening notes of
  Debussy's *Golliwog Cakewalk* to the first chords of *Song of
  Storms* from Legend of Zelda.

Uses:

To call everyone from around the house (the piano's sound carries
very well).

To get someone's attention even if they are in the same room and
they are not responding to their name (we are a family of super focused
people and often have a hard time stopping what we are doing or even
hearing someone who's talking to us).

To get someone to stop an annoying action (because once focused,
certain children have a really hard time hearing "stop" or "I don't like
that", but incorporating the piano call and then asking seems to do the
job).

To encourage quick obedience. I like to congratulate kids when they
respond right away. When I do the *everyone call* and a child stops
playing and shows up right away, I give that child extra time to play or
work on whatever they were focused on, before having to transition to
something new (if possible).

Note:

We do joke, especially with our oldest son, that he'll have to teach
his future wife his piano call. Now that we know more about the autism
spectrum, it is probably a good idea for all of the kids when they grow
up. I do want them to hear and answer to their names, but it will probably always be a bit of a struggle.

∾

Stoplight Thinking

This is another tool that is especially helpful for all of us.[1]

STOP
LIGHT
steps to
peace

STOP!
Freeze:
stop moving,
keep hands off people/things
Calm Self:
get away from stimulus,
breath, pray

THINK

What is happening?
What am I feeling and why?
What can I appropriately do?
Choose (include prayer).

GO

Go and do:
calmly
appropriately
get help

BONUS INGREDIENT: RECIPES

The book is named after a food, so we thought we'd better include some recipes. Here are some of our favorite and most-used recipes and cooking tips.

∽

Basic Salad Dressing
    1/2 cup olive oil
    1/4 c apple cider vinegar or lemon or lime juice
    1 tsp. salt

Then add other seasoning and spices. Usually:
    1 tsp. dried garlic
    1 tsp. dried onion
    1/4-1/2 tsp. cayenne

Then add one (or sometimes two) of the following (depending on what you are putting it on)
    1 tsp. basil

1 tsp. oregano

1 tsp. ginger

1-2 tsp. taco seasoning mix (this can substitute out for all the other spices above)

or try some other herb or spice

Shake in a jar.

≈

Oriental Dressing

1 cup olive oil

1/2 cup rice vinegar

1 Tbsp. sesame seed oil

1 Tbsp. soy sauce

1 tsp. garlic

1 tsp. ginger

sesame seeds

≈

Taco Seasoning (for salad dressings, tacos, and soups)

2 Tbsp. dried onion

4 tsp. chili powder

2 tsp. salt

2 tsp. dried garlic

2 tsp. cumin

1 tsp. cayenne pepper

1 tsp. paprika

≈

Basic Salad

We eat many variations of this recipe through the summer.

.   .   .

2 heads of romaine lettuce (or 4 romaine hearts), chopped
6+ tomatoes, chopped
½ pound spinach, chopped
1-2 cucumbers, sliced

Add a variety of the following veggies:
bell pepper
onion
avocado
apple
daikon/radish
jicama
celery
carrot
cauliflower
cabbage

Add one or more types of protein:
cheese: cheddar, mozzarella, or feta
beans: black, garbanzo, etc.
seeds: nuts or sunflower seeds
egg: hard boiled or scrambled
meat: hamburger, chicken, or pork

❧

Easy Salsa Salad
Chop and mix together:
tomatoes
cilantro
onion

diakon
salad greens

Sprinkle the following over the top, then mix in (keep tasting the salad, then add more of these ingredients if necessary until you like the flavor):

lime juice
olive oil
salt
pepper

∾

Basic Meat and Veggie Seasoning
These are basically the same ingredients as the salad dressing. Our kids know this ratio and change up the specific herbs and spices according to what sounds good for the day. We use this in stir fries and soups.

2 tsp. salt
1 tsp. dried garlic
1 tsp. dried onion
1 tsp. each of multiple herbs (this changes from salad to salad: basil, oregano, thyme... be creative)
1-2 tsp. of a spice (if using cayenne we do ½ tsp.)

∾

Quick Meals
These are our go-to meals when we are busy. Cherry, Pecan, and Apple can make these without any help. Lime and Huckleberry are getting close.

. . .

Hamburger Green Bean Stir Fry
    8 cans green beans
    1-2 lb ground beef
    1 large onion, chopped
    seasonings (see basic seasoning recipe)
    rice (brown or white)

Cook rice. In a frying pan, sauté ground beef and onion. Season. Add green beans. Serve over rice.

Cabbage and Egg
    1 head cabbage
    14 eggs
    soy sauce and something spicy (we often use cayenne and garlic)
    rice (brown or white)

Cook rice. Chop cabbage. Stir fry with oil. Mix eggs with soy sauce and seasoning. When cabbage is cooked, add eggs. Stir until cooked. Serve over rice.

Freezer Veggie and Bean fry
    3-4 lbs of freezer veggies (broccoli, carrots, and cauliflower is our favorite blend)
    3 cans of beans (or if we were planning ahead, home-cooked beans)
    seasonings
    rice (brown or white)

Cook rice. Cook veggies in a frying pan with several tablespoons of coconut oil, then add beans and seasonings. Serve over rice.

~

Other Family Favorites

(no recipes included, but maybe some of these will jump start a meal idea)

Sushi Salad: The ingredients of sushi but all tossed together. It is much quicker to make but has the same great flavor.

Sushi Burritos: They are like giant sushi rolls, including the seaweed wrap, and allow for a lot more ingredients. We don't make them often, but we sure love them.[1]

Nacho-Taco Salad: Cheese melted on tortilla chips and served with taco salad.

Chicken-Bacon-Apple-Cilantro Salad: Basic salad with these specific ingredients and a poppy seed dressing.

Borscht: A hearty soup that always has beets, but everything else varies. When I lived in Russia, I learned that there are as many types of borscht as there are families who make it.

Homemade Ramen: A homemade broth rich with the lovely flavors of ginger, garlic, soy sauce, and sesame. Cherry plans this almost every time she's in charge of the menu. Comfort food.

.   .   .

Scrambled Egg Muffins: Cheesy, eggy, and rich. Delightful with a side of veggies.

~

And a final favorite....

Burger Salad
Like a burger without the bun, and easier to eat than a lettuce wrap. Jesse said we had to include this recipe.

1 lb ground beef
1 large spoonful of coconut oil
1 onion, chopped
salt, pepper, and garlic powder to taste
3 cups day-old rice
12 eggs

Brown ground beef and onion together with coconut oil. Add seasonings. Add rice and heat through. Add egg and cook. Add more seasonings if needed.

1 large head romaine lettuce, chopped
4 tomatoes, chopped
4 large pickles, chopped
1 bell pepper, chopped
1 avocado, chopped

Mix together.

Dressing:
Pickle juice, sour cream, salt, mustard, ketchup (and if needed, a little olive oil and vinegar to bulk out)

. . .

Pour dressing over salad and let sit. Just before dinner, add the hot meat mix. Serve immediately.

~

OK. I can't end without a pie recipe. This is my Grandma's delicious pie crust, as shared by my cousin Jenny Harris.
   Thank you Grandma and Jenny!

Grandma Stewart's No-Fail Pie Crust[2]

INGREDIENTS
- 4 cups flour
- 1 1/2 tsp salt
- 1 Tbsp sugar
- 1 3/4 cup lard
- 1 Tbsp vinegar
- 1 egg, beaten
- 1-4 Tbsp ice water*

INSTRUCTIONS

- In a large mixing bowl, combine flour, salt, and sugar. Use your hands or a pastry cutter to add the lard. Mix until coarse crumbs form.
- Make a well in the center of the dry ingredients. Add egg, vinegar, and 1 Tbsp cold water. Mix together. Add enough additional water to form a slightly sticky dough.
- Divide dough into 3-4 portions and shape each into a disk.

Wrap each disk in plastic wrap and refrigerate for at least two hours before rolling out.

- Remove from refrigerator and let sit at room temperature for 20 minutes before rolling out. (Dough should be soft enough to roll out but not so soft that it becomes sticky). Makes three small or two large double-crusted pies.

Notes from Jenny:

*We usually just put a small bowl of water in the freezer when we start baking. By the time we need it, the water is well chilled.

Dough can be frozen for several months. Place plastic-wrapped disks in a heavy-duty Ziploc bag for freezing. Remove from freezer and thaw to room temperature before rolling it out.

UNTIL WE MEET AGAIN...

At the end of my typed journal, I have the words, "This is the end—*for now.*"

It is true. More will happen. Things will change. New vistas and new challenges will arise. Life is beautiful, complex, and rich. This is the end of my current experiences, where I'm at—for now, but not for always.

May your own journey be filled with daily joys and growing experiences. God bless you.

—Maria

APPENDIX: POEMS OF PRAISE

More poems on our Savior and His place in my life.

I Am

> Not "I was"
> Nor "I will be"
> But "I am"
>
> Christ "is" from
> before the world
> Creator
> Redeemer
> Advocate
>
> He is our source of
> Life
> Light
> Hope

Because He "is"
We can become.

—Inspired by John 8:58

Alpha and Omega

Alpha.
Beginning.
Before the world
He was.
Firstborn,
offering Himself
to fulfill His Father's plan.

Omega.
Ending.
Dying
to end death,
break bonds of hell.
Sacrifice.

Alpha and Omega.
The Beginning and the End.
Spanning eternity
so we may live.

—Inspired by Revelation 22:13

Hosanna – Save, I Pray

No unclean thing
can dwell with God.
We knew this when
we left heaven.

We also knew unless we left,
we'd never progress.

We needed bodies.
We needed mortality.
We needed to choose,
to grow, to change.

And we knew we'd
make mistakes.
We'd do things that would
make us unworthy to return.

God, in His perfect love
and infinite wisdom,
provided a Savior
to pay for us,
to cleanse us,
to save us.

The cost to His beloved Son
was our hurts, our sins,
born upon His back,
squeezing His heart,
until blood dripped from every pore

then to bear death,
so he could break the

bonds of death and hell.

He rose in glorious resurrection,
opening the prison.
Granting all resurrection,
and all a chance to
change and return home.

Hosanna, Hosanna,
to God and the Lamb
Who saves us!

—Inspired by 2 Nephi 9:10

The Light, Life, and Way

The Light
Light given to us at birth.
Light by which we see
right from wrong,
truth from error.

When all else is
dark and confusion,
remember to
look to the Light—
look to Christ.

The Life
First fruits of the
resurrection,
through Him all
will be resurrected.

And each broken person,
fractured by life and trials,
will receive a perfect body
through the gift of
the Life, our Savior.

The Way
He shows the only path to return to God,
to progress onto all the blessings
God desires to give us.

He says to us
"Come, follow me."

—Inspired by John 14:6

Teacher

He taught on the wayside,
in the courts of the temple,
among the outcasts and despised,
before kings.

He taught the truths of eternity:
our divine parentage,
why we came to earth,
how we may return
to our heavenly home.

He taught the higher law:
love thine enemy;
pray for those who
despitefully use you;

forgive thy brother.

Always He spoke the
words of His Father.
Always the words of life.

He taught by parable,
by stories, and perfect example,
allowing His listeners
to learn at their level of readiness.

Am I ready?
Will I learn?
He reaches out.
"Come follow me."

As a Hen Gathereth her Chicks

The once noisy barn lay silent.
Fire left black skeleton rafters.
Ribs of charred walls radiated heat.
Ash puffed with each step.

The farmer scanned the destruction.
He'd saved most of his animals.
That was blessing enough,
though the next year would be hard.

He kicked a blackened lump,
then leapt back as
three chicks scurried out.

A hen had gathered her chicks

under her wings,
protecting them from the fire,
even as she lost her own life.

—Inspired by Matthew 23:37, 3 Nephi 10:6

Shepherd Gifts

Wise men brought gifts:
gold, frankincense, and myrrh.

The shepherds brought gifts too:

immediate obedience
to go and see.

Humble worship
to a baby lying in a manger.

Shared testimony
to all.

I don't have gold, frankincense or myrrh to give.
But I can give gifts like the shepherds'.

—Inspired by Luke 2:15-17

CITATIONS

Slice 1: Geeking Our First Year

1. Anna Karenina by Leo Tolstoy

Baker's Tip: Lessons in the First Four Years of Marriage

1. I'm so grateful for my parents' teaching me this. It is a vital part of navigating life.

Baker's Tip: Parenting 201

1. https://www.churchofjesuschrist.org/share/what-is-general-conference?lang=eng
2. The Ensign is now called the Liahona. https://abn.churchofjesuschrist.org/study/magazines/liahona?lang=eng

Slice 12: Growing Up

1. https://www.churchofjesuschrist.org/study/liahona/2003/10/at-home-with-the-hinckleys?lang=eng

Baker's Tips: Lessons in Many Years of Marriage

1. *My Early Life* by Winston Churchill

Baker's Tips: Some Final Parenting Thoughts

1. https://www.churchofjesuschrist.org/study/scriptures/the-family-a-proclamation-to-the-world/the-family-a-proclamation-to-the-world?lang=eng

Ingredient: Faith in Christ

1. https://www.churchofjesuschrist.org/study/ensign/2000/04/the-living-christ-the-testimony-of-the-apostles-the-church-of-jesus-christ-of-latter-day-saints?lang=eng

Ingredient: Gratitude

1. Heard from someone wise. Thank you, whoever you are.
2. https://www.churchofjesuschrist.org/study/general-conference/2014/04/grateful-in-any-circumstances?lang=eng
3. *The Hiding Place* by Corrie Ten Boom

Ingredient: Covenants

1. https://www.churchofjesuschrist.org/study/manual/gospel-topics/covenant?lang=eng

Ingredient: Repentance

1. https://www.churchofjesuschrist.org/study/general-conference/2018/04/until-seventy-times-seven?lang=eng
2. *A House United* by Nicholeen Peck
3. https://www.churchofjesuschrist.org/study/general-conference/2020/04/13rasband?lang=eng

Ingredient: Forgiveness

1. https://www.churchofjesuschrist.org/study/ensign/2020/12/what-church-leaders-are-saying-about-forgiveness?lang=eng&id=title3%2Cp4-p5#title3
2. https://www.churchofjesuschrist.org/study/ensign/2020/12/what-church-leaders-are-saying-about-forgiveness?lang=eng&id=title3%2Cp4-p5#title3
3. My Battle with Religious OCD, Ensign, Sept 2019
4. CS Lewis, from a letter to Miss Breckenridge, 19 April 1951
5. https://www.ldsliving.com/Preventing-Pornography-Addiction-3-Ways-LDS-Families-Can-Help-Break-the-Shame-Cycle/s/87509

Ingredient: Respect

1. https://www.churchofjesuschrist.org/study/general-conference/2020/10/17oaks?lang=eng
2. Many of these ideas came from *Never Split the Difference* by Chris Voss.

Ingredient: Love

1. https://www.churchofjesuschrist.org/study/general-conference/2010/10/of-things-that-matter-most?lang=eng
2. https://en.wikipedia.org/wiki/Mao_(card_game)
3. Boundaries with Kids, by Dr Cloud and Dr Townsend

Ingredient: Work

1. I learned about "disagree appropriately" and other parenting skills from *A House United* by Nicholeen Peck
2. Box Hockey instructions: https://www.youtube.com/watch?v=1wVq_vpMf08&feature=emb_logo
3. https://www.theidearoom.net/block-puzzle

Ingredient: Education

1. I love this guidance: "Members of the Church should seek out and share only credible, reliable, and factual sources of information. They should avoid sources that are speculative or founded on rumor. The guidance of the Holy Ghost, along with careful study, can help members discern between truth and error."

    https://www.churchofjesuschrist.org/study/manual/general-handbook/38-church-policies-and-guidelines.title_number226-p2391?lang=eng#title_number226#title_number226
2. Wisdom from my parents.
3. https://www.odysseyofthemind.com/
4. https://www.churchofjesuschrist.org/youth/childrenandyouth/what-is-children-and-youth?lang=eng

Ingredient: Wholesome Recreation

1. https://www.deseret.com/2008/7/7/20262225/favorite-outdoor-games
2. https://www.physicaleducationupdate.com/public/471.cfm
3. https://groupactivityideas.weebly.com/smurf.html
4. Things as They Really Are, June 2010 Ensign, Elder Bednar

Bonus ingredient: Piano Calls and other Spectrum Tools

1. I've seen many different versions of this. For example: https://www.teacherspayteachers.com/Product/Stop-Think-Act-Poster-3821743

Bonus Ingredient: Recipes

1. https://www.feastingathome.com/sushi-burrito-recipe/
2. https://www.prosaiclife.com/2019/01/grandmas-pie-crust/

ACKNOWLEDGMENTS

Thank you to my loving parents who taught me in the ways of truth and righteousness. Everything I am started at home, under your tender nurturing.

Thank you to my husband and my children for many family discussions, joyful growing experiences, and your love.

Thank you to all my family who've read my many newsy letters over the years.

Thank you to Gail McMullin, Jessica Tessem, Claire Hill, Tori Gollihugh, Kimberly King, Louise Stewart, Kameo Monson, Samanth Stewart, and Vikki Meyer for reading drafts of *When I was a Pie.* Your suggestions helped me know what to thin out or elaborate on. I especially want to thank Jenny Harris for reading two vastly different versions of the book and providing valuable feedback both times.

Thank you to Cherry for creating the comics. For many readers, the comics are their favorite part of this book.

Thank you to my editor, Annie Douglass Lima. As always, your fine-tune edits brought a lovely polish to the book.

Thank you to Oladimeji Alaka for the lovely cover design. And to Jesse Farb for making modifications.

Most of all, I want to thank my Heavenly Father and my Savior, who have blessed me through every step of writing, and all other areas of my life.

ABOUT THE AUTHOR

What? You want to know more about the author? Here are five fun facts:

As a child, I couldn't walk across a room. I danced, spun, skipped, ran, or otherwise moved, but I couldn't just walk. (Huckleberry inherited that boundless energy).

I took calculus at a community college at age 14. I planned to go to MIT and become an astronaut. Plans changed—in wonderful ways.

As a youth, I made up stories to help my little sisters go to sleep. It backfired. We stayed up for hours continuing the tale. My first novel was born in those late, whispered nights.

I lived in St Petersburg, Russia, for half a year teaching English to kindergarteners. I learned to wash my clothes in a bathtub, filter and boil my drinking water, and love my sweet, crayon-eating kids.

I love writing! When I'm not writing family stories, I'm creating adventures, fantasy, fairy tale retellings, and poetry.

ALSO BY M. L. FARB

THE KING TRIALS
The King's Trial (also an audiobook)

The King's Shadow

HEARTH AND BARD TALES
Vasilisa

Fourth Sister

Heartless Hette

HEARTH AND BARD SHORT STORIES
Flight: A Vasilisa Novelette

Birth: A Fourth Sister Novelette

Gift: A Heartless Hette Novelette

FREE SHORT STORY
East of Apollo's Palace

FAMILY AND HUMOR
When I Was a Pie: and Other Slices of Family Life

Made in the USA
Monee, IL
21 November 2021